Passport to Fame

As Sonia in "A Kid For Two Farthings" (1955)

Passport
to Fame

The Diana Dors Story

Huw Prall

The Book Guild Ltd

First published in Great Britain in 2018 by
The Book Guild Ltd
9 Priory Business Park
Wistow Road, Kibworth
Leicestershire, LE8 0RX
Freephone: 0800 999 2982
www.bookguild.co.uk
Email: info@bookguild.co.uk
Twitter: @bookguild

Typeset in Aldine401 BT

Printed and bound in Great Britain by CPI Group (UK) Ltd, Croydon, CR0 4YY

ISBN 978 1912083 381

British Library Cataloguing in Publication Data.
A catalogue record for this book is available from the British Library.

For my beloved parents Mary & Ron who worked their socks off to give me a good start, whose love was unconditional and who always believed in me, even when I did not believe in myself.

Contents

Acknowledgements

I would like to extend my grateful thanks to a number of people who have contributed in one way or another to this book

Firstly the late George Baker who I had the privilege of meeting and who shared some of his reminiscences of Diana with me.

Murray Melvin, archivist at the Theatre Royal Stratford East for sourcing material on Diana's 1951 appearance there in the play "Miranda".

Keith of Alexander's Theatre Emporium for providing me with the wonderful Stoll Moss cards included giving a unique insight into Diana's variety performances.

Paul Sullivan who runs the official Diana Dors website and who put some wonderful photographs of Diana from her personal collection at my disposal.

Kate Lees and Richard Jeffs of Adelphi films and Vic Pratt from the British Film Institute who asked me to write a piece for the booklet included in the DVD release by the BFI of two of Diana's films "Miss Tulip Stays the Night" and "The Great Game", and for putting stills and information at my disposal regarding the four films Diana made for Adelphi.

Fellow Diana enthusiast David Almond who has provided me with both photographic and written information on Diana as well as sharing his own thoughts on her.

Thelma Town-Clear who set me off on my theatrical career and has constantly shown enthusiasm for this project and spurred me on.

The following people and companies have all helped me in one way or another, and apologies for any omissions: - Paul Buckingham, Callprint Dolben Street London SE1, Barbara Cruden, Dataprint Alton, Donald Darroch, Brenda Green, Susan Howe, Rona Kelly, Kwik Film London N12, Longworth Photographic Farnborough, Paul McCready, Kevin Minshull, Guy Minter, Eileen Nash, Mike O'Neill, Rob Pearce, Ryman Aldershot, Simon Sheridan, Yvonne Wilson, and to all my dear friends who have offered encouragement to me during the writing of this book.

Jeremy Thompson and his wonderful staff at The Book Guild whose knowledge and expertise have made this book possible Jack Wedgbury, Hannah Virk, Katherine Ward and Philippa Iliffe.

Finally a huge thank you to Dame Barbara Windsor DBE who kindly read some of the chapters and was so encouraging about the content.

Prologue

"To succeed in show business you need some basic ingredients – a lot of luck a lot of guts, a skin like a rhinoceros, and the patience of a saint – a little talent helps"

Diana Dors

14 January 2017 was a very special day in the Wiltshire town of Swindon. It saw the unveiling of a blue plaque to mark the place where one of the icons of British Cinema was born – the legendary Diana Dors.

Swindon Heritage Magazine campaigned for the plaque which marks the place of Diana's Birth on the site of the former Haven Nursing Home.

Diana Mary Fluck was destined to become a real superstar. After adopting her grandmother's surname of Dors, a true legend of the silver screen was born.

With a career spanning over 35 years, she was one of the most recognisable actresses of her time. With her immaculate long flowing platinum blonde hair, Diana was often referred to as the British Marilyn Monroe; but she was so much more than that - a well respected actress with an intelligent and powerful personality.

Diana tragically died too young. In 1984 she sadly lost her fight with cancer aged just 52.

This is her story.

Act One

1

Enter Miss Fluck

The maths lesson was really boring as far as Diana was concerned. What good were sums to you anyway if you were going to be a film star? She looked down at her exercise book, at the names of the film stars she had written in the margin – Judy Garland, Lana Turner. She had read in a film magazine that Lana had been discovered while sipping an ice-cream soda in a Hollywood drug store. Maybe the same thing would happen to her in the Kardomah coffee bar in Swindon's High Street.

She was awakened from her day dream by the angry voice of the schoolmistress asking what she was doing. Quickly she covered her exercise book with her hands, but was asked to uncover it immediately.

"Why have you not finished your sums Diana Fluck, and what is that written in the margin?"

"The names of my favourite film stars miss."

"Diana Fluck I don't know what is going to happen to you. All you seem to do is daydream. I don't know what your father will say if you don't show some improvement".

Diana scowled. Her father Bert would not be pleased. She could hear the familiar words

"What's the point of paying out all this money for a private education and then getting reports like this?"

However she knew her mother would defend her, pointing out that as long as she could add up the few pounds a week she was ever likely to earn it did not really matter!

Selwood House School was in the Bath Road, Swindon and was run by two sisters Miss Daisy and Miss Ruth Cockey. Bath Road young ladies were expected to be genteel and respectable, and Diana was not interested in being either. She had one clear goal in life and that was to be a film star.

From an early age she was taken to the cinema by her mother as often as three times a week. The beautiful women on the screen dressed in gorgeous gowns, courted by handsome men captivated the little girl, and would lead her to write an essay in the English lesson "What you would like to be when grown up". Diana's composition was clear and to the point. She was going to be a film star with a cream telephone and a swimming pool. The telephone seemed to be the epitome of glamour, and it is interesting to see that at the height of her career she very often had a cream telephone in her publicity photographs.

Young Miss Fluck never really got on with her father, and as she grew up she sensed he resented her more and more. She would learn, mostly from her 'Auntie Kit', that before she arrived, her parents had formed a close friendship with a young bachelor called Gerry Lack. The three were inseparable and always took their holidays together sometimes staying at Diana's Grandmother Georgina's cottage in Wales, but more often in fashionable Weston-super-Mare. Gerry Lack was never short of money, and Diana's father Bert was unfortunately off holding a good position in the accounts department of the Great Western Railway, which meant that her mother and Gerry spent a great deal of time in one another's company.

"Bert" or Albert Sidney Fluck to give him his correct title had been a handsome Army Captain when he first met his wife to be during the First World War. Mary was working in Swindon as one of the country's first post women. Originally from Wales, she had moved to Wiltshire with her husband William Padget and his family to find work. William enlisted when the war broke out and was killed in action. Bert met her at the post office where she worked.

He finally married her on 9 March 1918, and they enjoyed a solid, if unexciting, marriage. It came as something of a surprise when Mary found herself pregnant at the age of forty-two, and after thirteen years of their union. Diana Mary Fluck was born on October 23 1931 at the Haven Nursing Home in Swindon. It was touch and go for the infant as she had been struggling to leave the womb for over a week, and was black in the face through near suffocation, but as was to be the pattern throughout her life, she was a survivor against all the odds. When the baby was placed in her arms, Mary decided there and then that Diana would have everything that she had not.

Soon after Diana's birth, Gerry's visits abruptly ended, although he was present at her christening on 13 December 1931 as one of her godparents. Diana could never believe that her father could have been so naïve as to what had probably occurred between her mother and Gerry Lack. As she said in her autobiography 'Dors by Diana' in 1981:

"Whatever happened between her and 'Uncle' Gerry – subsequently my godfather – I will never know. But as I see it, my destiny was woven by two men: one of whom grew tired of my mother when I arrived on the scene and went in search of another; and one who, although legally my father yet completely unsuspecting as to the reality of his fatherhood, was extremely jealous of my presence and never really came to terms with the fact that his wife's affections were now centred on her child. Maybe this was the cause of my own feelings for and my rejection of him, or maybe it was a deep-rooted, subconscious knowledge that perhaps he was not my real father. Whatever the truth it is lost in time, for only my dear mother knew what came to pass before I was born."

Although Diana did not shine at school, she did excel at out of school activities, instigated by her mother. Firstly dancing classes, and at the age of five, elocution lessons. By the time she was six, she was winning first prizes in competitions in her home town and this resulted in write ups in the local papers, none of which impressed her school heads. "Your conduct in class is the only thing we are interested in" was the usual comment made.

With the outbreak of World War Two in 1939 Diana, at nine years old, found herself going with her father to many of the concerts he organised for the troops. An accomplished pianist, he would often accompany Diana in her rendition of such perennial favourites as 'The

Good Ship Lollipop' and 'Ma I miss your Apple Pie", when one of his team of amateur entertainers let him down.

The war dragged on and with it came a new and exciting phase in Diana's life. She was going to meet some real American men! It was 1944 and with the approach of the allied invasion of Europe known as D-Day, thousands of them were coming to Britain. Because of limited accommodation at the camps and barracks around Swindon, anyone who had a spare room was being asked to accommodate one or more GIs. The Fluck's had a spare room and Diana's excitement knew no bounds when she discovered that their particular American came from California. She bombarded him with questions about her favourite stars which he did his best to answer, but as his family owned an orange farm about a hundred miles north of the film capital, he was hardly in a position to satisfy a young girl's thirst for information about Tyrone Power and Lana Turner.

At twelve and a half Diana had taken to wearing make up. Her hair was long and by the aid of some lightener was honey coloured. She was regaled with cries of "Hey it's Veronica Lake" by the GIs as she sauntered around the streets of Swindon, and this in turn led to invitations to dances where she pretended to be seventeen, and looked every inch of it in her real nylons and semi high heeled shoes.

Towards the end of the GIs stay in Swindon, Diana and her parents went to Weston-super- Mare for their annual holiday. Whilst there she entered, aided by her doting mother, a beauty contest to find a pin up girl for Soldier magazine. Bert, of course, was not consulted. Giving her age as the usual seventeen, she paraded around the swimming pool in a scarlet and white swimsuit with red high heeled shoes and trying to look as much like Betty Grable as possible. She came third. Posing for photographs afterwards by the swimming pool, Diana's feet in white court shoes were placed as elegantly as any film star's.

As the picture was going to appear in the Swindon Advertiser, and as part of her prize was a photo shoot for Soldier magazine, her father had to be told of her success. Bert was not pleased, but had begun to realise that if he put his foot down she would only be more determined, and with his wife aiding her, he was on a hiding to nothing. Secretly he believed she would grow out of her ambition to be on the silver

Beauty contest at Weston-super-Mare (1945)

screen, and settle down to a nice secretarial job with the Great Western Railway. How wrong he would find he was!

The picture in the Swindon Advertiser was spotted by a professor of art at a nearby college which had been opened for servicemen whose studies had been interrupted by the war. She was offered work as a life model a few times a week at a fee of a guinea an hour, her first paid engagement. A few weeks before Diana's fourteenth birthday, when she became the University's official pin-up, she mentioned that her ambitions went beyond modelling and that she wanted to become a great actress. She was found a place on the college drama course, and went on to appear in several productions. She played Emily in a play called "One Week in Paris" and then Grazia in "Death Takes a Holiday", which was greeted as the success of the month.

All of these achievements fired Diana up even more to reach her goal in life – to be in front of the film camera – and she began investigating courses at Drama schools. She knew her father would be against it, so developed a clever strategy. On the understanding that she would study for a teaching diploma and return to Swindon to teach elocution, Mr Fluck gave his daughter permission to attend the London Academy of Music and Dramatic Art (LAMDA). Thrilled at the prospect of studying at a London college, Diana travelled up to the metropolis once a week, accompanied by her mother where she undertook private acting classes with Miss Kathleen Cunningham.

Shortly after the start of these weekly trips another piece of good fortune came her way. An American photographer she knew at the college in Swindon, gave her a letter of introduction to a film director he knew in London. The letter was to a Mr Keating who at the time was involved with a film called 'This Man is Mine" starring Glynis Johns. The studio where the film was being made was in Islington and on one of the weekly trips to LAMDA, Diana and her mother visited him. She was captivated by the excitement of the film studio, and observed Mr Keating rushing about and giving orders. Perhaps Margaret Lockwood, the top British film star of the day, had actually stood on the same spot as she did now. The letter was handed over and Mr Keating read it politely and said he would do what he could to help.

It wasn't until much later that she was to discover he was only an assistant director, and had less influence in the industry than a main director. She was downhearted on the meeting day, as with the enthusiasm of youth, she expected something to happen immediately. However it was an introduction after all, and most importantly she had taken her first steps into the magical atmosphere of a real film studio. Things were looking up, but there was a disappointment just around the corner; the Americans were returning home. Swindon seemed a duller place.

There was no time to lose. She was fourteen years old and time was running out. If she was to achieve her ambition of stardom in Hollywood something would have to be done. After a lot of persuading her father allowed her to attend LAMDA as a full time student rather than a part time one, but still on the understanding that she would train as an elocution teacher. Diana's acting teacher Miss Cunningham and her elocution tutor Mrs Barraclough had both stressed that this was an area in which she really shone.

2

Drama School And Screen Tests

January 1946 saw Diana on Swindon station with a green suitcase and a return ticket, with the promise made that she would return home every weekend. Her father had given strict instructions that she was to work hard as failure was unthinkable. To her young and ambitious mind the thought of hard work did not enter into it. Why should it? She was training to be a glamorous film star and how could it be hard to achieve something she had always wanted?

When she arrived at Paddington station she saw an advertisement on a large hoarding of Margaret Lockwood, Britain's No 1 screen actress, advertising Drene Shampoo 'The Shampoo of the Stars'. Diana said to herself "one day it will be me up there advertising Drene". Another ambition which would come to fruition. Diana was to stay at the YWCA hostel which was just around the corner from LAMDA and would ensure her welfare was taken care of.

At seven the next morning she was awakened from sleep by a loud bell. Half an hour was given to get washed and dressed, then down to breakfast. Classes at LAMDA commenced at ten. At fourteen she was the youngest full time student the Academy had ever had. Diana took to college life like a duck to water – stage make-up, improvisation, film technique, Shakespeare and other classics, miming and fencing, as well as the all important speech training.

The earlier meeting with Mr Keating bore fruit around this time as he contacted the Gordon Harbord Agency to say that she was a likely young girl for films, and Mr Harbord became her agent. The now classic film 'Black Narcissus' was being cast at this time, and Diana was summoned to Mr Harbord's office to discuss a role in it. To her horror she discovered the part which she envisaged was not glamorous at all, but that of a wind tanned Nepalese girl. With youthful exuberance it never occurred to her that she would not get the part. The role would eventually be given to the young Jean Simmons.

This was a setback, but another opportunity was just around the corner.

Through the help of a photographer on her home town newspaper 'The Swindon Advertiser' she obtained an evening job as a model for London's Camera Club. The inevitable happened and she was asked to pose nude. Her mother was consulted who in turn conferred with her father. Bert Fluck was resigned by this time to the fact that Diana would go her own way in life and so said it was entirely up to her. Diana therefore divested herself of her clothing for the fee of one guinea an hour, a considerable amount in post-war Britain.

The training regime at LAMDA was rigorous and the students were required to gain their Bronze, Silver and Gold medals culminating in a diploma before their graduation. (It is interesting to note that in later life Diana would be a professional adjudicator for LAMDA's Licentiate Acting Diploma.) Diana had been awarded her Bronze medal by Peter Ustinov, and now she was working for her Silver. The adjudicator was a Casting Director Eric L'Epine Smith. For the exam Diana performed pieces from 'As You Like It', 'While Parents Sleep', and 'Wuthering Heights'. At the end of the examination the adjudicator called her out into the theatre auditorium and told her that she had not only passed, but that he had awarded her the medal with honours. There was even more exciting news to come.

Mr L'Epine Smith explained that he was casting a film 'The Shop at Sly Corner' which had been a big London stage success, and that there was a small part in it for which he felt she would be perfect. There was, however, a slight complication and this had nothing to do with her acting abilities, but her age. The role to be cast was the girlfriend of the villain in the story, and the character was a little older than Diana's fourteen years. He went on to say that for the time being he would keep her age quiet, and when she was given her screen test to say she was seventeen.

Diana was ecstatic. A Screen test! At long last she was on her way. The screen test took place at Wharton Hall studios, Isleworth, and Diana sailed through it. George King the director was delighted and Mr L'Epine Smith even more so at the success of his 'discovery'. Later he did give her real age to the director who refused to believe it because Diana was so convincing in the part. The young actress's salary was fixed at £8 a day, and the contract was drawn up by her agent Gordon Harbord. The only problem as far as he was concerned was her name – Diana Fluck. It was felt that people might vulgarise the surname and so an alternative needed to be found. The agency came up with Scarlett, after the heroine of 'Gone With The Wind'. She had also used the name Carroll as a model. It was her mother who came up with her stage name. Dors was her grandmother's maiden name, and she felt that it sounded good to have two names starting with the same letter. So Diana Dors it was.

'The Shop at Sly Corner' had been adapted from Edward Percy's stage play and starred Oscar Homolka, Muriel Pavlow, and Derek Farr. Diana played the part of Mildred, the cheap, tarty girlfriend of Archie Fellows, played by Kenneth Griffith. Her big scene was a good dramatic one and she grabbed the opportunity with open arms. The role took three days to complete, and on her return to LAMDA Diana found she was treated with a certain amount of awe. The Principal Wilfred Foulis also saw her in a different light, for he had up until then viewed her in the same way as her father, that she was a rather silly young girl who didn't want to accept responsibilities and would probably come to a no good end! She was now taking steps to prove both her father and the principal wrong.

Some weeks later she received a call from her agent asking if she could jitterbug. Needless to say she could. All the dancing she had done with the Americans back in Swindon had given her experience in this crazy dance. The film was called 'Holiday Camp' and was being shot at the Gainsborough studios. The story line would introduce the 'Huggett Family' and Diana would go on to have an important role in

Diana as Mildred with Kenneth Griffith as Archie in
"The Shop at Sly Corner" (1946)

Diana attends a screening of her second film "Holiday Camp" (1947)

two of the three films that were to be made about them. This however was in the future. Now Diana took herself down to Gainsborough studios to dance the jitterbug with actor John Blythe, who would play her boyfriend, then husband in the future Huggett films. She was engaged for one day at the princely sum of £10.

Diana's third film was soon to follow. Called 'Dancing with Crime', it featured Richard Attenborough in one of his first starring roles. The story involved a murder at a dance hall. Her character 'Annette' worked there as a hostess. Filming took place at Southall studios in February 1947 and it was during this period that she came to realise that the glamour of the film studio was almost non existent. One of the effects that the war had on London was a series of shortages. This included a number of power strikes in one of the coldest winters Britain had known for nearly fifty years. The result of this was that when everyone arrived at the studios at 6.30am, frozen and weary, make-up would have to be applied by the light of a candle! For the dance hall sequences Diana was in an elegant but cold evening gown, off the shoulder and backless. She was at least able to wear slacks underneath it!

Her day began at 4.30am when she arose at the YWCA, then made her way down the seventy eight stairs to the dining room where a bowl of cornflakes had been left out for her breakfast. A walk then followed up Lexham Gardens and into the Earls Court Road, where she kept strictly to the middle for fear of someone jumping out and attacking her. On arrival at Earls Court underground station a combination of trains and buses got her to Twickenham studios. All very different to Hollywood where the sun shone constantly.

Her salary for 'Dancing with Crime' was again £10 a day and she was paid in cash at the end of each day. By the end of her five weeks filming she had amassed about £150. When she went home that weekend she proudly showed the money to her parents. Mr Fluck was a little bitter commenting that it was ridiculous that a fifteen year old girl was earning more money than he was!

After her third film it was back to LAMDA and more hard work. The culmination of the training at this particular drama school was to obtain the Gold medal and diploma. At the end of term the principal awarded her the 'London Films Cup'. This had been presented to LAMDA by

Diana as Annette with Richard Attenborough as Ted in
"Dancing With Crime" (1947)

Sir Alexander Korda. The presentation was made in the academy's own theatre, and in front of an invited audience. For publicity purposes a leading film actress – Greta Gynt – was invited to present the award to the 'girl most likely to succeed in British films'. Little did Diana know that she would soon work with Greta Gynt. Her father had written her acceptance speech which concluded by her saying that she would "keep the banner of LAMDA flying high in the world of films".

"The Shop at Sly Corner" was released and Diana was able to see herself on the screen for the first time which she described as "an incredible experience!" When the film was shown in her home town of Swindon there was considerable publicity for their own 'Diana Dors'. The posters put up around the town all featured her name and she was asked to make a personal appearance at the opening. Her father acted as her escort on the night and had written a speech for her to deliver from the stage of the cinema, which she did, dressed in a silver sequin trimmed white evening dress and beaver lamb coat which had been bought by her mother.

Diana had barely returned to LAMDA for the summer term when she received a call from her agent asking her to go to Gainsborough Studios to do a screen test for Sidney Box for a forthcoming film "Streets Paved with Water", starring three up and coming British actors – Maxwell Reid, Jane Hylton and Andrew Crawford. The screen test resulted in Diana being given fourth lead in the film playing Jane Hylton's bad sister. The part was a very showy one and many people said she would steal the film. However after a months filming Diana arrived at the studios one morning to be told that through studio politics the film was being postponed for a while. In actual fact the production would never be completed.

This was obviously a blow to Diana, but the screen test also provided her with another positive, namely J Arthur Rank offering her a ten year contract. The weekly salary began at ten pounds a week, rising in stages until it reached three hundred pounds a week at the end of the ten years. Rank, of course, had a yearly option on renewing the contract. The Rank contract signed, Diana's first pay cheque was paid into a bank account by her father. He said he would handle all the money to ensure that she used it wisely.

Publicity portrait for the abandoned
"Streets Paved with Water"

Student Production at LAMDA

Halcyon Days with fellow LAMDA students.

3

Rank Starlet

David Lean had received serious critical acclaim in 1946 with the release of his screen adaptation of Charles Dickens' "Great Expectations". He now had a new project in the offing, a screen version of "Oliver Twist" to be made at Pinewood Studios. Lean wanted to test Diana for the role of 'Charlotte', the sluttish daughter of the undertaker and his wife. For the test her face was smeared with dirt and she was dressed in ragged Dickensian clothes. A far cry from being another Betty Grable she thought, but the kudos of working for a first class director such as David Lean more than made up for this.

Upon completion of 'Oliver Twist', the Rank Organisation sent Diana to their training school for young actors. This was based at their studios in Highbury, North London. 'The Company of Youth' as it had originally been called was the idea of producer Sydney Box. The rationale behind the organisation was to train new stars for the screen. Subjects covered included, of course, acting, but in addition deportment, elocution, stage and screen technique, make up and dress sense. To someone like Diana who had already had a drama school training, this was going over old ground, and from what one reads in various publications, not taught so well either. However as many of the Rank starlets had been discovered in beauty pageants with no theatrical training behind them it did fulfil a useful purpose. David Henley, head of the contract artistes department at Rank had merely sniffed when

As Charlotte in "Oliver Twist" (1948) with Kathleen Harrison,
John Howard Davies and Michael Dear.

Diana had informed him of the awards she had won at LAMDA, and she began to realise that medals and diplomas meant little in the outside world.

The task of training new stars for the Rank Organisation was in the hands of Miss Molly Terraine, a former silent movie actress. She firmly believed that a sound knowledge of stage technique was vital before entering on a screen career, and for that reason, when the potential stars had had their elementary training at Highbury, they were sent to Worthing to appear in repertory for a month.

Diana hated everything about the 'charm school', as it was christened by one press critic, especially the weekly cocktail parties which they were forced to attend to meet producers, directors and other influential people in the industry in the hope of getting themselves cast in some film or other. Many of those at the charm school faded into obscurity but there were a number of successes in British cinema including Susan Shaw, Christopher Lee, Pete Murray, Barbara Murray, Dermot Walsh, Hazel Court and Bill Travers. Diana of course was one of the successes and was released from the school to appear in small parts in a number of films in 1947.

In 'Good Time Girl', at the time a controversial film starring Jean Kent, she appeared as Lyla Lawrence. Her scenes were played opposite Flora Robson who Diana described as "that magnificent actress"

'It's Not Cricket' starred Basil Radford and Naunton Wayne, who had found fame in Alfred Hitchcock's 'The Lady Vanishes'. Diana had an amusing scene where she applied for a job in their office.

'The Calendar', a racing drama, was based on a novel by Edgar Wallace. In this she played 'Hawkins', a prim uniformed maid. Diana served tea to Greta Gynt who had presented her with the cup at LAMDA.

'My Sister and I' starred Sally Anne Howes and Martita Hunt, and was a murder mystery set around a provincial repertory company. Diana was a young girl in pigtails delivering a script to Sally Anne Howes.

Molly James was the character Diana played in 'Penny and the Pownall Case' and was one of her first substantial roles. This was made at Highbury studios, home of the 'charm school'. Her character

As Lyla Lawrence with Flora Robson as Miss Thorpe in
"Good Time Girl" (1948)

was secretary to a senior police officer. Diana hated working on this film, mainly because they cut her lovely thick hair, because she said the hairdresser could not be bothered to dress it each day. When she complained about this she was reprimanded by Molly Terraine. "What kind of actress do you call yourself? Do you think Laurence Olivier enjoys walking around Denham with dyed blonde hair while he's playing Hamlet?" Diana thought this a rather stupid comment. He was after all the star of what was going to be a huge picture, whereas 'Penny' was definitely a second feature!

Sydney Box now came up with her biggest screen role to date. The film 'Holiday Camp' in which she danced the jitterbug had introduced a family called 'The Huggetts', and Gainsborough pictures were now planning a series of films featuring the family. The first was called 'Here Come the Huggetts' and Diana played the glamorous but flighty cousin who comes to stay while her mother is in hospital, and completely disrupts the family. She would also appear in the follow up film 'Vote for Huggett'. The actor she played opposite was John Blythe who had been her dance partner in 'Holiday Camp'.

Diana felt her career was really progressing well until she attended the press showing of 'Here Come the Huggetts' with her mother. They both thought the film extremely funny and laughed heartily. Afterwards the atmosphere in the foyer was not good to say the least. After this she made a point of never attending one of her own press shows again.

There was another film just around the corner. Diana was summoned to Gainsborough studios by director Ralph Smart, who was just about to start work on a film about cycling clubs called 'A Boy a Girl and a Bike' which was to be filmed mainly on location in the beautiful Yorkshire dales. Diana was to be billed as top supporting actress. Patrick Holt, John McCallum, and Honor Blackman were the leads. Filming was to begin in two weeks time. Prior to this the producer Ralph Keene gave a cocktail party at his home in Chelsea to give the cast an opportunity to meet one another. Diana felt she was riding on the crest of a wave meeting so many well known stars.

The big day arrived to depart to the Yorkshire dales. A private car picked Diana up to take her to Kings Cross station where she was to meet the producer who was going to escort her and a young actor called

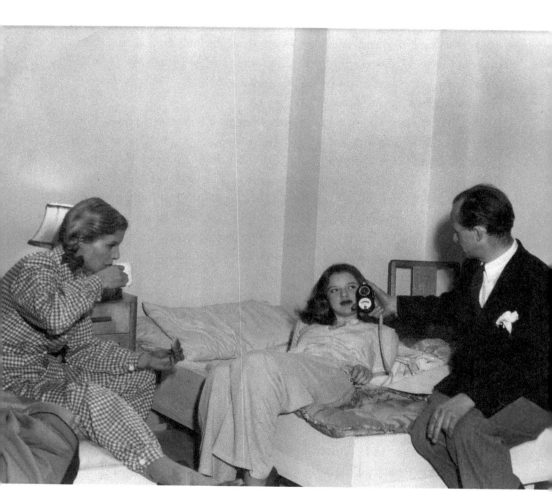

Undergoing technical checks with Peggy Evans on the set of
"Penny and the Pownall Case" (1948)

Signing autographs for young fans

Every inch the Modern Miss in "Here Come The Huggetts" (1948)

Anthony Newley on the journey. As the two youngest contract players with Rank and therefore valuable properties, it was not felt they should make the journey alone. Anthony Newley had turned in a brilliant performance as the artful dodger in 'Oliver Twist', but his and Diana's paths had not crossed during filming as her few days shooting had taken place on the dingy undertaker's set.

The Yorkshire dales were beautiful and Diana found herself falling in love. Egil was a tall handsome nineteen year old Norwegian cameraman, the brother of Greta Gynt. On return from the idyllic Yorkshire setting, Diana felt she could no longer stay at the YWCA and continue her romance with 'Gil'. So much to her parents horror she set about finding a flat. She found a furnished one just off of the King's Road, Chelsea for a rent of five guineas a week. Sadly for Diana the romance was not the same in London. She wondered if he was married or had someone else, but he assured her that this was not the case. Gil suggested in the end that they cool things for a while. So Diana found herself alone, and then unexpectedly Anthony Newley confessed that he loved her. They began associating with the fast Chelsea set and Diana's flat became a meeting point for out of work actors and late night parties.

Just around the corner was her biggest break. David MacDonald, a director with a rather wild reputation, was preparing the first British Western – 'Diamond City'. The stars were to be David Farrar, Honor Blackman and Jean Kent. Honor Blackman was to play a Salvation Army girl and Jean Kent the part of a hard bitten saloon hostess. However Jean was tired of continually playing bad girls and declined the part. Diana was tested and immediately cast. The screen test involved a love scene with David Farrar. Afterwards the director commented "there's no way she could have played that scene if she was still a virgin!" Diana was fired with enthusiasm at the prospect of working on this film. She knew it would interfere with the busy social life she was now leading since her move to Chelsea, but was determined to be self disciplined and felt that her career as an actress was the most important thing in her life.

As Ada Foster in "A Boy a girl and a Bike" (1949)

4

The Dandy And Diamond City

Christmas 1948 was spent with her family at her Auntie Kit's home in Cardiff. Aunts, Uncles and Cousins she had not seen for many years were there, all of them keen to see their famous relative who they already regarded as a 'star'. Diana did her best to be enthusiastic but all she really wanted was to return to London.

New Years Eve found her back in London spending it with friends in the Cross Keys Pub. In the crowded smoky atmosphere Diana was to see a man whose eyes seemed to pierce right through her. His name Michael Caborn-Waterfield, later to be known as 'Dandy Kim'. He was quite an arrogant young man which Diana found intriguing. When she told him of her role in 'Diamond City'. he just informed her he was off to Hollywood which, like so much of his life, was an unreachable dream. Most of his time was spent selling anything he could get his hands on, and spending the money quickly due to his very extravagant lifestyle. Diana was fascinated by him and they began seeing one another regularly. Michael lived with his friend Patrick Beresford in St John's Wood, and she would visit him with her studio stand in Oona, who began dating Patrick.

This new love interest in her life resulted in Diana losing some of her dedication to acting and she spent her evenings with Michael in clubs and bars usually falling into bed around 4am, rising at 6am to be taken by studio car to Denham where filming of 'Diamond City' was taking place. This lifestyle however took its toll on her health, and one day she collapsed at the studio. The film was nearing completion fortunately, and the producer had her taken home to Swindon and her mother's care. Calls from Michael to her home were frequent during this period, but her mother believed this was just another passing infatuation.

Fully recovered, Diana returned to London where a shock awaited her. The lease on her flat was to be terminated. Michael and his friend Patrick Beresford were also in difficulties in St. Johns Wood. Patrick had been relying on some inheritance coming through. There were now problems with this, and the result was that they could no longer afford the flat. Their plan was to buy a share in a funfair situated in Swanage, Dorset. Things were changing all round as far as Diana was concerned. She found a small flat in Jermyn Street, just around the corner from Piccadilly Circus. It was a depressing apartment and the only way she could see the sky was by putting her head out of the window. Before Michael left for the new venture in Dorset, he presented Diana with a beautiful engagement ring, a topaz set in gold.

It was now the summer of 1949 and, as Diana was not filming, the Rank Organisation sent her to the Connaught Theatre in Worthing to appear in "The Cat and the Canary' with Barbara Murray. Diana's mother accompanied her. She had disapproved of her daughter's relationship with Michael and had told her so in no uncertain terms, so it seemed an ideal opportunity to spend a relaxing few weeks together. Unfortunately whenever Michael called, her mother immediately became hostile again. As Diana's parents had predicted, the fairground venture floundered, and on her return to London Michael moved into Jermyn Street with her.

With still no film work on the horizon, Diana was again sent out by the Rank Organisation. This time to appear opposite Marcel Le Bon in a musical called "Lisette". She was feeling unwell all the time with constant nausea, and the reason was soon apparent; she was pregnant. The producer of the play somehow found out, and when Diana asked to be released from performing, he threatened to tell not only the Rank Organisation but her parents as well. In post war Britain there were only two options open to an unmarried woman in this situation. One was to go away discreetly until the baby was born and give it up for adoption, the other was far more risky – an illegal abortion.

DOLPHIN THEATRE

BRIGHTON

WEEK COMMENCING

MONDAY, 19th SEPTEMBER, 1949

LISETTE

A NEW PLAY WITH MUSIC BY

DOUGLAS SARGEANT

Programme 6d.

"Lisette" (1949) with Marcel Le Bon,
Claude Bailey, Renee Reel and Paul Anstee

Somehow Diana managed to get through the play and returned home. Investigations were made and a woman was found in Battersea who would terminate the pregnancy for the sum of ten pounds. The problem was how to raise the funds. In the end Michael contacted his stepmother and asked her outright for the money, even explaining to her what it was wanted for, much to Diana's surprise. The whole episode was extremely painful for her, not just the physical aspect of the termination, but the emotional scars it was to leave. It took her many months to recover.

"Diamond City" was released to poor reviews, but this did not diminish Diana's excitement at seeing her name in lights in Piccadilly Circus. Her next film assignment was for Ealing Studios in a production called "Dance Hall". Two of her co-stars had featured in the earlier Huggett films – Jane Hylton and Petula Clark. Oona was still dating Michael's friend Patrick, and her fortunes were about to change, as he was to receive an inheritance of £18,000. Michael was to come of age the following year and was convinced his inheritance would be far in excess of this sum. At this time both he and his brother John just received an allowance each week of the princely sum of two pounds from their stepmother.

The spring of 1950 saw Diana appearing in the play "Man of the World". This was produced by a young man – Kenneth Tynan who had come down from Oxford. She was to receive excellent reviews for her part and "Theatre World" magazine voted her "Actress of the Year". The cast included a young actor called Lionel Jeffries who was to become a close friend. The summer was to bring little professional work apart from a week in an American play "Born Yesterday" which was performed at the Kenton Theatre in Henley on Thames, one of the smallest and oldest working theatres in Britain. The rest of the time was spent on a round of parties.

Diana's parents were going on holiday to Paris that summer and called to see her en route. Luckily Michael was not present, but several actor friends were lounging around the flat which drew the comment from her parents that they were "fair weather friends". As far as Diana was concerned at nineteen life was to be enjoyed, so their comments were ignored. However she was soon to realise the truth of them

Practicing the Can Can for "Diamond Ciry" (1949)

LYRIC THEATRE - HAMMERSMITH

Lessee: Associated Theatre Seasons Ltd.   Licensee: J. Baxter Somerville

Telephone: Riverside 4432

WEDNESDAY, FEBRUARY 22nd, at 7.0

Evenings at 7.0   Matinees: Thursday and Saturday at 3.0

TENNENT PRODUCTIONS LTD.
(in association with the Arts Council of Great Britain)
presents

ROGER   URSULA
LIVESEY   JEANS

IN

MAN OF
THE WORLD

By C. E. WEBBER

DIANA DORS
(By permission of the J. Arthur Rank Organisation)

MICHAEL BALFOUR   **GEOFFREY EDWARDS**
ERIC POHLMANN   **MICHAEL GODFREY**

DUNCAN LEWIS

WALTER GOTELL   **BARTLETT MULLINS**
LIONEL JEFFRIES   **GEORGE MITSIDIS**

WYNNE CLARK

Directed by KEN TYNAN
Setting by REECE PEMBERTON

**A COMPANY OF FOUR PRODUCTION
FOR A LIMITED SEASON**

when she was summoned to the offices of the Rank Organisation and informed that because of loss of revenue some contract artistes were being released; one of which was herself. Suddenly the realization hit her, there would no longer be any weekly pay cheque coming in, which although it had not been a fantastic amount, had been adequate for her and Michael to live on.

5

Life After Rank

Diana landed a part in another film "Worms Eye View" which earned her a fee of £250, but because of the mounting debts this was soon eaten up. Michael's twenty first birthday was approaching and they both looked forward expectantly to his inheritance. When New Years Day arrived, the envelope from Michael's stepmother brought only disappointment. A cheque for £50 and a note explaining that as business affairs had deteriorated she could do no more, but she would continue with the £2 a week allowance to him and his brother John.

The estate agents asked them to vacate their flat immediately and early 1951 saw them getting their belongings together. Before they left John turned up on the doorstep also broke, asking to borrow Diana's transistor radio to pawn it. An unpleasant exchange of words followed and John left. Looking out of the window she saw him getting in to a blue American convertible. Someone was already in the car waiting and Diana asked casually who it was and received the reply from Michael "oh some fellow called Dennis Hamilton". The name was to become a very important part of her life.

February 1951 saw Diana back in the theatre at the Theatre Royal Stratford East playing the title role in "Miranda" – the story of the mermaid by Peter Blackmore and directed by Phyllis Gow. Previously it had found fame as a film with Glynis Johns playing the lead. The next few months saw them relying on the hospitality of friends. They

"Miranda" Theatre Royal Stratford East February 1951
with Denis Gordon (Goacher) as Charles.

"Miranda" Theatre Royal Stratford East
February 1951

"Miranda" Theatre Royal Stratford East February 1951 with Michael
Darbyshire as Paul Marten and Jean McConnell as Clare Marten

eventually settled in a bed sitting room in a residential club in South Kensington. Diana's career appeared to have come to a complete halt, then she was approached about the possibility of going to Broadway to appear in the play "Springtime for Henry" by Ben Levy. This immediately fired her up with enthusiasm. Going to America at last. She suffered the agonies of waiting for many days, and then received a call with the producer's decision that the project was off. So it was back to waiting around for something to happen, and, quite without warning,it did.

She received a call from Gordon Harbord to say that Frank Launder and Sidney Gilliat were screen testing for the lead in a new film called "Beauty Queen" which would eventually be released with the title "Lady Godiva Rides Again". Diana made her way to Shepperton Studios and gave her all for the benefit of the director. Unfortunately they did not feel she was quite right for the part, as they wanted someone more naive and inexperienced. However they did offer her the part of the beauty queen's friend "Dolores August" who was an old hand on the beauty circuits. She was engaged for the sum of £800 which was spread over eight weeks, and a guarantee of top feature billing. The film saved the day for Diana as the remuneration paid off most of her debts. When the film unit went on location to Folkestone she was feeling much happier with life.

The offer of another film was just around the corner from a company called Exclusive Pictures, later to be known as Hammer Films. American actor George Brent was coming over from Hollywood to star in "The Last Page". The part Diana was offered – Ruby Bruce – was a good dramatic one and for the four weeks work she would receive a salary of £450. Around the same time Michael was to get himself into trouble over a shady perfume deal he had become involved in, and was awaiting a court appearance when Diana began her location filming in Folkestone for "Lady Godiva". Upon her return to London, filming continued at Shepperton Studios, and as she was not required to be in attendance every day Diana found herself with time on her hands. One afternoon she visited the S&F Restaurant in Piccadilly. Here she was to meet the man who would change her life. His name – Dennis Hamilton.

"Lady Godiva Rides Again" with Pauline Stroud

Diana was sitting with an actress friend – Jennifer Jayne and in her book "Dors by Diana" relates how "an extremely handsome young man at the next table leant over and asked for a light". The result of the meeting was that Dennis settled the bill for tea and Diana accompanied him to the Palladium to see Danny Kaye – "his incredible ice blue eyes compelled me to do just as he said". He was not the usual type Diana was attracted to – black curls and dark brown eyes. His eyes were blue and his long and curly hair was dark brown. The attraction came in the form of his personality. He had done many things to earn a living including being a small part actor and stand in for British film star Eric Portman. He told Diana that he had given this up because he was useless at it, and also wanted to eat regularly. She was to comment that in spite of all his confidence in life, put him in front of an audience or camera and he froze.

After the performance at the Palladium they went on to a club where they discovered they had much in common, including sharing the same birthday. After this meeting she felt sure he would contact her again although he knew she was living with Michael. When he did contact her she introduced him to Michael who was not overly impressed by the new man on the scene. With his court case approaching he was understandably apprehensive and playing games was very low on his list of priorities. He had good cause to be concerned. On the day of the hearing Dennis offered to drive Diana and some of her friends to the court. The judge sentenced Michael to two weeks imprisonment, to Diana's considerable distress.

Dennis grabbed this opportunity with both hands and made his move on Diana. When she returned from the studios each day flowers would be awaiting her accompanied by pieces of poetry. Diana felt pangs of guilt as she still had strong feelings for Michael, but then something happened which began to make her doubt the feelings he had for her. She met a girl who claimed that Michael had been making love to her while Diana had been working. Dennis took advantage of the vulnerability she was experiencing and proposed marriage. In her turmoil of emotions she accepted him.

6

The Spider And The Fly

As Diana was a minor she had to have her parents consent to marry, but this was not the problem she anticipated. Her parents had never approved of Michael and were relieved to see her getting away from him, so their consent was given, over the telephone. The marriage was to take place at Caxton Hall. Michael in prison was of course unable to do anything about the forthcoming ceremony himself, but he arranged for a friend to telephone the registry office, and inform them that the signatures of Diana's parents on the consent form were forgeries. Upon their arrival at Caxton Hall Diana and Dennis were met by an official who took them to a private room and informed them of the call. According to Diana, Dennis grabbed the man by the throat and threatened to knock his teeth down his throat if he refused to marry them. Needless to say the ceremony went ahead! The unpleasantness of the experience increased Diana's self doubts as to whether she had done the right thing. Michael was soon to be released. She had lived with him for almost two and a half years, and here she was married to a virtual stranger.

Diana was now filming "The Last Page" and Dennis was selling water softeners. While at the studios she was able to keep in touch with Michael secretly. He was planning to go off to France but needed some money. Diana full of guilt agreed to give him most of the money she was earning on the film to help him in his new life on the continent. The result of her actions revealed another side of Dennis which unnerved Diana. As he called her a faithless whore, Diana found herself thrown from one side of the room to the other by Dennis, and punch followed punch. He then rang her parents in the middle of the night and gave a full rendition of how she had been unfaithful with Michael. This whole experience was to make Diana view him differently from then on. She now knew that there was this incredibly generous side to him, but also the Dennis who flew into uncontrollable rages and would simply not listen to reason.

The producer of "The Last Page" was a Mr. Robert Lippert. He had been impressed by her performance in the film and wanted to offer her a Hollywood contract at the incredible sum of four hundred dollars a week. His plan was to build her up as a British version of Shelley Winters. However there were a few problems that needed to be sorted out first, the main one being that Diana was married. When he met with her agent Gordon Harbord, he stipulated that she must get a divorce. With the glamorous build up he envisaged for her, being married was hardly going to enhance it. Gordon Harbord tried to explain that we did not do things like that in England. Mr. Lippert was not interested. He suggested that Diana should divorce Dennis, and then marry him again at a later date, which he reasoned would make great publicity. Dennis of course was furious when Diana related the story to him, but there was a reprieve as the producer had to return to America.

With filming on "The Last Page" completed and Dennis' water softener company failing, they found themselves almost completely without funds. No work was on the horizon for Diana and she was getting more and more depressed over this. The only hope she had was the offer of the Hollywood contract, but this was to fall through when the producer had a falling out with the American Screen Actors Guild. She really felt that this was the end of all her hopes and aspirations, but Dennis assured her that he was going to make her into the greatest star Britain had ever known. He put these plans into action immediately by telephoning each national newspaper with the story that Diana had turned down the offer of a Hollywood contract because she wanted to remain, and make all her films, in England. The fact that she had no offers on the horizon made not one jot of difference to Dennis' way

"The Last Page" with Peter Reynolds

of thinking. To Diana's amazement the press accepted the story, and Dennis predicted that the offers would come rolling in, but of course they did not.

A few more opportunities were just around the corner however. The BBC approached her with a view to appearing in a television comedy series called "How Do You View" which featured comedy actor Terry Thomas. During rehearsals she received a call from her agent informing her that Burt Lancaster was in London and preparing a film called "His Majesty O'Keefe". He was interested in meeting her to discuss the possibility of a part in this, but Diana was doubtful that she would get the role as it was that of a native girl in the South Sea Islands. Buoyed up with Dennis' predictions of stardom she went along to Claridges to meet him. A few months later she was given a screen test, but as she predicted Diana failed to get the part, and it was won by an up and coming young actress called Joan Rice.

During this period they were living in Dunsfold very near to Guildford in Surrey, but with bills piling up with the local tradesmen, they decided to move back nearer to London and settled in Esher. A further sadness now followed for Diana as she discovered she was pregnant. With the current situation they found themselves in, a child was out of the question and she was to find herself again on the receiving end of a termination.

Celebrating passing her Driving Test with husband Dennis.

7

Rendezvous With The West End

As with so many downs in life it often happens that an up will follow, and around this time a producer contacted Diana with a view to her appearing in a revue he was hoping to mount at London's Comedy Theatre. On the way to the interview to discuss the show Diana was to acquire a status symbol which would guarantee her good publicity. They were driving an old Opel at this time, and as they passed a garage with several cars for sale, Dennis spied a black Rolls Royce, and immediately declared "we're going to buy that". Diana of course could not believe what she was hearing, her main concern being how they were going to pay for it. Dennis however dismissed all her objections, went into the manager's office at the garage, and ten minutes later emerged with all the paperwork completed, proudly announcing they were now the owners of a Rolls Royce.

The wheels of publicity were rapidly turning in Dennis' head as he formulated his plan to announce that at twenty she was the youngest owner of a Rolls in the country.

Diana won the role in the revue which was called "Rendezvous", and although the show itself was not a great success, she herself received considerable praise from the critics. As is often the case success generates more success and she found herself the recipient of many offers of work. Laurence Olivier wanted her for his forthcoming film "The Beggars Opera", and she was offered a summer season in

Blackpool with Bebe Daniels and Ben Lyon in "Life with the Lyons" for the then huge sum of £100 a week. A variety agent also approached her with a view to her putting together a twenty minute variety act to tour around the music halls. He estimated that she could earn herself £135 a week with this. Diana politely declined the offer, informing him that she was primarily an actress. He replied that the offer would always be open to her.

After the closure of "Rendezvous" at the Comedy, she appeared in a modest little film called "My Wife's Lodger" before heading off to Blackpool, where she had decided to accept the summer season with the Lyon family. She did not really care for Blackpool but the £100 a week made the prospect of the three month work schedule bearable. When the Blackpool season ended Diana returned to London with Dennis where they rented a small house in Chelsea. Another film was to follow: "The Great Game" featuring Thora Hird and James Hayter. Dennis himself appeared in it, in a small cameo role as her boyfriend.

As Diana's career went from strength to strength both professionally and financially, many people saw her as an actress being controlled by a dominant man. She was in later life to comment how she felt "stifled and cornered like the cat's captive mouse". Having seen the bad side of his personality Diana felt frightened of Dennis. Although he was protective of her, sometimes she felt he was over protective. Another offer of a West End production shortly followed. "Remains to be Seen" had run on Broadway and was being presented in London by impresario Jack Hylton. Although Diana had an agent, Dennis negotiated her weekly salary of £175.

During the rehearsal period Diana celebrated her twenty first birthday, as did Dennis. A joint party was held at their Chelsea home, and it was during this that Diana began to have more doubts about him. Due to an early rehearsal call, Diana went to bed while the party continued downstairs. She was awakened by raised voices and went to look down the stairs to discover what was happening. Dennis was shouting and fighting with a friend of his who had had more than enough to drink. She heard the man say

"I'll tell Dors the truth about you! I'll spoil your meal ticket", and

COMEDY THEATRE

PANTON STREET, HAYMARKET, S.W.1. Phone: WHI 2578

Sole Proprietor: G.C.T. (Comedy) Ltd. Licensed by the Lord Chamberlain to H. H. Wingate
Lessee: Bernard Goodman Productions Ltd.

EVENINGS at 8-0 Matinee : WEDNESDAY at 2-30
SATURDAY at 5-30 and 8-30

By arrangement with BERNARD GOODMAN
HAYWOOD & RICHARDSON LTD.
By arrangement with LEMKOW BROS Ltd.
present

★WALTER CRISHAM
★DIANA DORS

ROBERTA CHILI
★HUBY · BOUCHIER★

in

RENDEZVOUS

A NEW INTIMATE REVUE
with

ROBERT JOHN
DORNING MARTIN

SARA LUZITA & TUTTE LEMKOW

KEITH CAMPBELL
and

★ARTHUR YOUNG

From the Norwegian book of Finn Bøe
English Adaptation, lyrics and additional music by MICHAEL TREFORD
Music by JACK LEMKOW
Produced by TOR LEMKOW

Echo Press Ltd., Loughborough

then Dennis punched him in the mouth. These words remained in her mind, but she tried hard to make herself believe that the accusation did not refer to the number of women he played around with in her absence.

The play toured for a few weeks before opening in London at Her Majesty's Theatre. Unfortunately it received a severe slamming from the press and critics and closed after just five nights which was a personal blow for Diana as she had received good reviews for her own performance.

HER MAJESTY'S THEATRE

HAYMARKET, S.W.I

Licensed by the Lord Chamberlain to PRINCE LITTLER
General Manager   FREDERICK CARTER

JACK HYLTON

presents

DIANA DORS   DICKIE HENDERSON JNR.

in

REMAINS TO BE SEEN

by HOWARD LINDSAY and RUSSEL CROUSE

(Authors of "Call Me Madam", "Life with Father" etc.)

DIRECTED BY RICHARD BIRD

Setting by George Ramon

First Performance : Tuesday, 16th December, 1952

MON., TUES., THURS. & FRI. EVENINGS AT 7.45
WEDNESDAY & SATURDAY AT 6.0. AND 8.45

THERE IS NO CHARGE FOR THIS PROGRAMME

8

Variety And Pantomime

She needed to find something else, and quickly. One afternoon as they were driving back to their apartment in Chelsea via Sloane Square, Dennis grabbed Diana's arm and pointed with excitement as he had spotted famous film director Sir Carol Reed, and exclaimed "That will be the day when you make a film for him, that will make them all sit up and take notice of you". Little did Diana realise that this prophecy was to come true.

However dreams were one thing and the practicalities of life, such as money, was another, and they were getting rapidly short of the latter. An agent offered a five week booking at some of the largest variety theatres around the country, starting at the famous Empire, Glasgow; a venue to strike fear in the hearts of seasoned veterans, let alone a totally inexperienced variety performer!

At every performance Diana wished the earth would open up and swallow her. However she felt better at the end of the first week when the manager presented her with her percentage salary of £250, the most she had ever earned for a week's work. By the end of the week she had re-arranged most of her act and the rest of the tour went more smoothly. Following Glasgow, she moved on to Birmingham, Portsmouth and Hull, gaining in experience and earning lots more money!

To Dennis this was far better than acting, but of course it was not really what Diana wanted, as she was above all an actress who needed others to work with on stage when performing. Despite Dennis saying there was more money to be made in variety, she could still earn good from her film work.

Her first film of 1953 was a comic farce called "Is Your Honeymoon Really Necessary?" and starred her with Bonar Colleano. For this she earned £1000 for three weeks work. She was then offered the same amount to appear with Frank Randle, a once famous but now fast declining northern comedian, in another film entitled "It's A Grand Life". In her autobiography "Dors by Diana" she described the film as "a complete and utter shambles". Randle was usually drunk and was often firing guns at the walls in his dressing room, as well as dragging girlfriends along corridors by their hair! Filming was constantly delayed because of his drunken binges, and this was to lead to Diana appearing in court.

It's A Grand Life (1953) with John Blythe and Michael Brennan

On one of the occasions when filming came to a halt, Dennis and Diana made their way to Blackpool to meet up with some friends they had made the previous year when Diana was appearing in "Life With The Lyons". On Saturday 18th July they checked into the Mayfair Hotel and called a few people inviting them over for a party. One of these, a man called Frank Rogers, was out, so Dennis, Diana, and a jeweller – Freddie Markell, went round to his flat. When they arrived he was still out, but Dennis managed to open a window which Diana was able to climb in through and let the others in via the front door. They remained in the flat for half an hour but still he did not return. Dennis got bored. He helped himself to half a bottle of wine, half a bottle of gin and a bottle of vermouth, which he gave to Diana and Freddie. As they left he scribbled a note to Rogers "we shall be drinking and getting pissed at your expense tonight. Waited over an hour for you. We thought we would leave you some wine". He also added a sketch of Rogers having sex with a naked woman.

Rogers returned home at midnight but did not notice anything until the early hours of the morning when he opened his drinks cabinet. Shortly after this Dennis called him inviting him to the Mayfair, but he refused. It was then that he discovered the note. He became very angry, and made a formal complaint to the police. Next day, Diana, Dennis and Markell were arrested on charges of breaking and entering and theft. Subsequently, following a court appearance, the two men were fined, but because it was her first offence, Diana was given a complete discharge.

The court appearance of course resulted in a wealth of newspaper publicity, which Diana hated but Dennis lapped up. Headlines such as "Diana Dors on Housebreaking Charge", and "Starlet Arrested" upset her parents a great deal , and they also received anonymous phone calls before the news hit the papers that their daughter had been arrested in Blackpool. Thankfully the whole thing blew over, filming continued on the Frank Randle fiasco, and they returned to the new home they had recently bought in Chelsea.

Diana's next film was already in discussion and very much in keeping with her recent "criminal activities". It was to be a strong drama about women in prison and based on a book called "Who Lie in

Gaol". This had been written by a woman called Joan Henry who had herself spent eight months in prison. Technical advice on the film was sought from Mary Size who had been a governor of Askham Grange, an open prison in Yorkshire. The film was called "The Weak and The Wicked", and Diana's co-star was Glynis Johns.

Diana's character – Betty Brown was a young woman who had been sent to prison for covering for her boyfriend's crimes. It was a departure from the usual type of role she was offered, and made use of her serious dramatic capabilities. Diana seized the opportunity of playing a girl in prison with no make up and enjoyed every moment of the film. The role was to bring her a fee of £1,000 so the future did not look too bad.

When shooting finished Dennis arranged a whistle stop tour of London cinemas to promote "Is Your Honeymoon Really Necessary?". Diana disliked the usual kind of personal appearances she had had to make when at the Rank Charm School, and so audiences were given a reprise of her act from "Rendezvous". Usually it involved appearing at two cinemas each evening, and the formula was that Dennis would first go on to the stage to introduce her, she would appear on stage and they would run through a question and answer sequence, then would follow her "Little Miss Muffet" routine from "Rendezvous" in which she recited the nursery rhyme in seven different dialects.

At this time Diana was also asked to do a radio series which she had previously appeared on from Germany the previous year, "Calling All Forces". Comedian Bob Monkhouse and partner Denis Goodwin were engaged as writers for this latest series. Monkhouse's humour and intellect reminded Diana very much of Anthony Newley and this was one of the guiding factors which attracted her to him. The attraction was mutual and was able to develop on Sundays when they spent the whole day at London's Garrick Theatre broadcasting the show, and away from Dennis and his suspicions.

However, she should have known how Dennis' mind worked by now, for a few weeks after the show ended, during a dinner party at the house, Dennis threw a fit and smashing most of the contents of the house up, accused her of doing all sorts of things with Monkhouse. A few weeks later he would go crazy again, when Diana, arriving in

Diana making a personal appearance in 1953

Bournemouth to appear in pantomime, was to receive an enormous basket of flowers with a long message from Monkhouse.

November 1953 saw a further extension of Diana's repertoire with the release of her first record "I Feel so mmm" / "A Kiss and a Cuddle". Sheet music was also produced for each song with her image on the covers.

The end of 1953 saw another "first" for Diana with her first venture into the aforementioned pantomime. She played the lead in "Aladdin" at the Boscombe Hippodrome, Bournemouth. She was offered the role by "Wee Georgie Wood" who was playing Widow Twankey, and the weekly fee was £250. Diana felt she was hopelessly miscast as she was probably the first blonde Aladdin to enter the magic cave.

Pantomime was a new learning curve for Diana. She found the rehearsals chaotic, and no one seemed to know their lines or moves to perfection, which she was used to in the "straight" theatre, but after the first three performances on Boxing Day, she began to realise that all this did not matter at all as the children in the audience loved every minute of the show.

Up until this time she had always felt very tense when doing her variety act, feeling completely thrown if anything had gone wrong. In the pantomime things were going wrong all the time and nobody seemed to bother, and gradually Diana found herself ad-libbing easily and talking to the audience as if she hadn't a care in the world. And even if it did all look terrible, it gave her great confidence in front of a live audience, which was to remain with her throughout her career.

Dennis was also in the pantomime playing a Chinese policeman as they were one short, and he was at the theatre every night with Diana anyway. He had one line to say "here comes Widow Twankey with her laundry basket" but all his confidence disappeared when it came to delivering his one line. This was the strange thing about him, thought Diana – in real life he had the impudence to say and do anything, but put him on a stage or in front of a camera and he was completely lost and nervous, which was clearly why he had never pursued his early career as an actor in spite of his good looks. He spent most of his time at the theatre playing jokes on Wood and other members of the company, or creating havoc at the hotel after the show.

Although Diana was to join in the laughter with everyone else, she felt empty inside because she realized there was no future for her and Bob Monkhouse. She always felt they would have made a great team with Bob writing scripts for both of them to appear in on television or in films. Following the end of the pantomime run, Dennis and Diana returned to London and more variety dates followed.

HIPPODROME - BOURNEMOUTH

An F.J.B. THEATRE
Direction : F. J. BUTTERWORTH
BOX OFFICE OPEN DAILY

(BOSCOMBE ARCADE)
Manager : W. PERCEVAL
Telephone : BOSCOMBE **362381**

FULLY LICENSED REFRESHMENT BARS

Commencing Boxing Day, Saturday, Dec. 26th
THREE SHOWS AT 2 p.m., 5 p.m. and 8 p.m.
& THEREAFTER FOR A SEASON OF FOUR WEEKS AT
2-30 p.m. AND 7-30 p.m. DAILY

THE FAMOUS SCREEN - STAGE - RADIO - TELEVISION STAR

DIANA DORS
AS
"*Aladdin*"

9

Sir Carol And Two Farthings

The early part of 1954 saw Diana doing a solo act at various variety theatres around the country. Music Halls were on the decline with the advent of television, and Dennis decided it was time to make as much money as possible from a dying form of entertainment. Dennis toured with her, and Diana was beginning to feel more and more stifled. She was constantly being compared to Marilyn Monroe, but often wondered how Marilyn would have coped with her life, which included grubby dressing rooms in such glamorous places as Huddersfield and Wolverhampton, while Marilyn had a beautiful suite at Twentieth Century Fox studios. Yes her life was very different to Marilyn Monroe, yet all the time she had to live up to that image. She was not jealous of Marilyn, but just felt that comparisons were unfair. However, her big chance was just around the corner.

"The Weak and The Wicked" had its premiere in February 1954 and received very good reviews. Picturegoer magazine ran an article "Dors Deglamourised" which praised her for taking on a role which was so different from her usual public image.

"Like Mae West, Diana has a good, honest earthiness about her performances – off and on stage – that makes a sharp contrast to the milk and water personalities of many young players. She gives the impression of having lived … Call her blatant, call her tough, call her anything you like. But can you *ignore* a character like Diana?"

As Betty Brown in "The Weak and the Wicked" (1954)
with Glynis Johns as Jean Raymond

Publicity still for "The Weak and the Wicked" (1954)

Diana was to continue with her variety tour for the first six months of 1954. In spite of the excellent reviews for "The Weak and The Wicked", no further film offers had followed. This did not stop her acquiring a new agent and one of the best to boot – Al Parker, who had many British Film stars on his books, and had a reputation for getting the best deals for his clients. In addition she gained a new agent for her variety work – Joe Collins, the father of actress Joan.

The next film that was to come along proved to be a flat stagey murder mystery, "Miss Tulip Stays the Night". Her co stars were Patrick Holt, with whom she had worked on "A Boy, A Girl and a Bike", and the husband and wife team Jack Hulbert and Cicely Courtenidge. It certainly did not stretch Diana's acting capabilities, nor do anything to enhance her artistic credibility.

Just before filming started on "Miss Tulip" she received a call from her new agent Al Parker with the news that director Carol Reed was casting for his forthcoming film "A Kid For Two Farthings". It was to be a light drama set in London's Petticoat Lane, telling the story of a small boy who buys a one horned kid goat which he believes to be a unicorn with magic powers which can grant wishes.

Diana was one of a number of young actresses being considered for the young female lead, the girlfriend of the young man who worked as a tailor's assistant and was also a body builder. Having been seen by Carol Reed, she had to wait ten days before she heard that she had the part. Asking his reason for casting her he replied:

"I had seen a lot of her films and thought she was right for the part. I ran them through again – and I was sure. I think she has a fine sense of comedy – and I also wanted a girl who could act. Diana is a nice little actress."

Diana was of course delighted at the recognition of her capabilities. She was after all a classically trained actress. As she said to the press "This is some league I'm in. Oh I know certain people look down their noses at me because I have worked in variety and I can wiggle when I walk and I like living a full life. But let them laugh now."

Her joy knew no bounds, and her salary for the film was fixed at £1,700. To be selected by Carol Reed was a great accolade for Diana and made many in the film industry take a fresh look at her. This included

"Miss Tulip Stays The Night" (1955) Diana as Kate Dax
with Patrick Holt as Andrew Dax

"Miss Tulip Stays The Night" (1955) with Jack Hulbert as P.C. Feathers

the Rank Organisation who renewed their interest in her by offering a new seven year contract worth £100,000. On Al Parker's advice the Rank offer was turned down, as he was confident that Diana would have much more success as an independent actress, rather than a contract one. Diana herself could see the sense of this. She could clearly see that had Rank not terminated her first ten year contract it was unlikely that she would have been able to enjoy the luxury lifestyle that was coming her way.

Success followed success and an offer came from producer Raymond Stross to appear in a cameo role in a film directed by J Lee Thompson called "As Long as They're Happy" and starring Jack Buchanan. The fee for this was £200 a day. Dennis immediately put this new found wealth to use by buying the house next door and renovating it for resale. By the time filming started on "A Kid for Two Farthings" in August 1954, he had persuaded Diana to move again, this time to a huge house by the Thames in Bray, with five bedrooms, a tennis court, and a boathouse by the river. It cost £7,000. A home fit for a star. In her autobiography "Dors by Diana" she herself describes this period with Dennis as "our happiest together". Away from the hustle and bustle of London they were to come to know peace.

Diana found working on "A Kid for two Farthings" a joyous experience. The whole production was of a high professional standard. The writers, producer and actors were all dedicated to the work they were doing and were not in it merely for the money. She felt very satisfied to be working in a calm and professional manner after some of the chaotic productions she had previously worked on. The experience of working with Carol Reed was something she would never forget. Having a major role in the film meant that virtually all her scenes were filmed under his close supervision.

However something occurred at this time which was to be a slight blot on the landscape so to speak. About a year previously she had posed for a photographer who worked under the name of "Roye" for a portfolio of 3D glamour photographs. The book was published under the title "Diana Dors in 3D" and was sold with a pair of cardboard glasses for viewing the photographs. It was issued as part of a series of similar books and was billed as "Stereo-Glamour Series 3". The pictures

"A Kid For Two Farthings" (1955) with Joe Robinson

of her were typical of the glamour material of the time and showed a skimpily clad Diana with the vital parts of her anatomy covered with pieces of chiffon and fur and even a toy tiger.

On 7th September, Halifax magistrates made an announcement that they were intending to prosecute John Gray, a fifty three year old shopkeeper, for possession of sixteen "obscene" titles including "Diana Dors in 3D". Mr John Bastian prosecuting said "How can a picture publication of a British film star scantily clad – a detective said she was practically nude! – be described as anything other than obscene? Coming into the hands of any person, it can have nothing but a corrupt and depraving influence!"

The Halfax magistrates retired for a month before reconvening. James Pickles, later to become Judge Pickles, represented the book's publishers, Trans-Atlantic Authors of Lamb's Conduit Street in Holborn, London. He asked the magistrates not to destroy the books on grounds of artistic merit, and the chairman extended the reprieve to the book and the other fifteen titles, although he said that some of them came very close to obscene.

However, by then the damage had been done. "Halifax Magistrates say Diana Dors is obscene" and similar headlines did not please Sir Carol Reed who was hailing Diana as his leading lady, and neither did it please Diana. To make up for the unhappiness it caused her, Dennis took her to Paris for her twenty- third birthday.

10

1955 The Golden Year

1955 was to be one of the most successful years of Diana's career beginning with a starring role in "Value for Money" for J Arthur Rank. Her co-star was John Gregson, the fee £5,000. On top of this the Rank Organisation invited Dennis to lunch to discuss another contract – this time on Diana's terms. Dennis came away with a five year agreement and no options, whereby she would be paid £7,000 a year to make only one film per year for Rank. In addition Dennis secured a contract for himself as a producer for Rank Films. However as Diana commented in "Dors by Diana":

"As with so many things, he never followed this through. It wasn't just that he knew his limitations were confined to promoting publicity stunts or making property deals. He could never concentrate on anything for any length of time."

During the filming of "Value for Money" Diana was invited down to the exclusive Pearl Harbour Yacht Club in Dorset to help judge a fancy-dress contest, and it was here that she discovered Dennis' infidelities. He took off in the car with a model one night when he thought she was asleep and she heard him go. An hour later he returned and Diana saw him get out of the car with the model, making it quite obvious that they had been enjoying one another in it. Diana spoke out about the matter and a terrible row was the result during which Dennis actually punched her in the face.

Fashion publicity for "Value For Money" (1955)

Fashion publicity for "Value For Money" (1955)

Dennis was very contrite after this altercation and showered her with presents, but it was no good. To quote Diana herself – "it was no good treating me like a child whose nursery must be filled with playthings. I was not a child. And yet I didn't feel like a real woman either!"

Even more sadness was just around the corner as in April 1955 Diana's mother. Mary, was taken into the Masonic hospital for a hernia operation. All went according to plan but Mary returned home in a much weakened condition. However she began to show signs of improvement and Diana began to think all would be well. It came as a terrible shock then when three weeks later, at the age of sixty five, she passed away.

Diana was devastated. She attended the funeral in a kind of daze, not really believing that the coffin being lowered into the grave actually contained her mother. Her father was heartbroken and the wreath from him and Diana simply said "From your Peter and our Diana."

Diana had little time to grieve as she was scheduled to do another film for Rank, which they had re-scheduled due to her bereavement. "An Alligator Named Daisy" was a slapstick comedy and her co-stars were Donald Sinden, Jeanie Carson, and James Robertson Justice. The director was J Lee Thompson who had directed her in the prison drama "The Weak and the Wicked". Diana was hoping he would remember her when casting his next forthcoming prison drama "Yield To the Night". Diana threw herself into the filming, and tried to show interest in Dennis' latest venture, a coffee bar in Maidenhead.

The summer of 1955 was to see two very important events in Diana's life. The first was the Venice Film Festival. The other Rank Organisation stars flew there, but Diana arrived in her new powder-blue Cadillac convertible. This caused a great stir amongst the Italian press, and even more publicity was to follow when she was photographed travelling down the Grand Canal in a mink bikini. Pictures of this now legendary outfit would be published all around the world.

A year later a new British musical called "Grab me a Gondola" starring Joan Heal opened in London, and told the adventures of starlets and a star – Virginia Jones – at the Venice Film Festival. One of the musical numbers was called "Mink" where the girls all sported mink bikinis.

Diana at the "El Toucan" coffee bar

During the festival it did not escape Diana's notice that Dennis also had an adventure of a rather different kind with the actress Mary Ure. On the evening of the British film and party, Dennis made a breathless appearance just before Diana's entrance and began to boast to anyone in earshot that Mary was his latest conquest.

On the return to England, Diana was to discover that she had been placed as the only woman among the top ten box office stars. The other good news was that "A Kid for Two Farthings" had received excellent artistic notices. The premiere which had been some months before was a glittering affair at which Diana received praise from Sir Laurence Olivier for her performance. The next great event for Diana was being presented to Her Majesty Queen Elizabeth II at the Royal Command Film Gala.

The sad factor in all this for Diana was that her mother had not lived to see the glowing success she was now achieving. After all her mother's dreams for her, she had just died a few months before she would have seen them realised. However, Diana was very relieved that her mother could not see the kind of life she was now living with Dennis.

J Lee Thompson kept his word about the starring part in his next film, the prison drama "Yield to the Night", and Diana was contracted to the lead female role of Mary Hilton. To this day people refer to the film as the story of Ruth Ellis, the last woman to be hung in Britain, but it had actually been written two years before she committed her crime. The story had originally been penned by Joan Henry who had written the previous prison drama Diana had appeared in "The Weak and the Wicked". Diana played Mary Hilton, a pretty young shop girl who falls in love with a nightclub pianist – Jim. He has another girlfriend, a smart society woman called Lucy, who basically is just using him, and eventually finishes with him. Jim in the depths of depression commits suicide and Mary cold bloodedly shoots Lucy to avenge his death.

There was much speculation at the time as to why Diana should have been picked for the role as opposed to more serious actresses such as Margaret Leighton, Ingrid Bergman or Vivien Leigh. Diana talking of director J Lee-Thompson's casting of her to the press said "Perhaps it's just that they've got so much more that I have. They're all wonderful dramatic and emotional actresses. But maybe people think of me as an ordinary girl, and when this terrible thing happens to an ordinary girl, it's more poignant. But you should ask the director, J Lee-Thompson. When he offered me the part I didn't say, "Why me?" – I just said, "Yes, please!" At last I've got the chance to play a real human being and not just a cardboard character with curves."

The film had originally been put forward to Rank, but the company had not been keen due to it's controversial theme, and it ended up being backed by an independent production company Associated British. Diana had signed a non exclusive contract with Rank so they were powerless to stop her appearing in the production, and the board of directors looked on horrified when the first pictures of Diana were published minus make-up and hair bedraggled.

The filming began at Elstree Studios in October 1955, but a week's delay occurred when Diana was involved in a car accident on the way to the studios. Dennis was unable to take her, so Diana decided to go to work in a hired car. Instead of sitting in the passenger seat or behind the driver, she curled up in the middle of the back seat and went to sleep. When the car slammed into the back of a lorry she awoke suddenly, seconds later her head slammed into the back of the front seat and she was simultaneously showered with glass from the smashed windscreen. An ambulance arrived and she was taken to Hillingdon Hospital. Doctors wanted to put stitches in the wound on her head, but it would have meant shaving part of her hair. After much pleading on Diana's part, they used plastic skin instead. Before Diana went back to the studio she celebrated her twenty fourth birthday a day early on Saturday 22 October, and on the Monday she was back on the set at Elstree Studios.

Journalists who visited the studio found Diana positive and approachable. The head of publicity at Elstree – Leslie Frewin – brought a group of writers to the set one day to see one of the dramatic climatic scenes being filmed. There were two rehearsals and the actual take went perfectly. One writer – Derek Walker – asked J Lee-Thompson if he felt it was fair to expect her to expose herself like this to a group of critics. The director replied "A lot of stars wouldn't do it, but with Dors it's different. I think she is, if anything, different with an audience. She likes to have a reaction to her performance."

Dennis had not been keen on Diana taking the part of Mary Hilton because for most of the film she would look tired and plain. Diana however was adamant that this was just the sort of part she needed to take on board, and in her heart knew it was the sort of part her mother would have liked to have seen her in.

At the end of filming Diana sat back and eagerly waited for the film's release. She had put her heart and soul into the part and everyone on the film had given over one hundred percent to the production. She knew it would come as a big surprise to many people who still thought of her as the dumb blonde which Dennis Hamilton had created.

For most of the shoot Dennis had not been around as he had been looking after his business interests. The coffee bar was bringing in £100 a week now which was a big help when filming engagements were not in the offing.

Diana was now beginning to feel that Dennis' Svengali hold on her was beginning to loosen, for she no longer needed his publicity gimmicks to make her a household name. Dennis was also beginning to feel a sense of unease. Yes, he was thrilled at the fame and money success had brought her, but there was also the fear of being left out in the cold if he was no longer needed.

On the set of "Yield to the Night" with Michael Craig
and Director J. Lee Thompson.

11

Show Business Personality Of The Year

Early in 1956 Diana was awarded one of the highest accolades in the show business world, when the Variety Club of Great Britain named her "Show Business Personality of the Year". A film columnist present at the ceremony was to later anger Dennis by describing him as a "suede-shod Svengali" and of Diana he wrote "I watched the expression on her face when he was not looking. She seemed so sad".

Some evenings later at a private dinner party at the house Dennis stormed "how dare that bastard call me a suede-shod Svengali". During the rest of the evening he became more and more inebriated and accused Diana of various infidelities. As the evening wore on Diana became tired and angry and to avoid any more altercations she went upstairs to bed. At around midnight there was a ring at the front door. It was two newspaper reporters also somewhat inebriated and demanding an interview with her. "Dors," Dennis shouted up the stairs. "Come down here, there are two pressmen who want to see you".

Furious at everyone's behaviour Diana called down the stairs that she saw no one at midnight especially when they called giving no notice. Dennis stormed up the stairs and into the bedroom. "You'll do as I say and come down and see the press" he yelled, grabbing her and propelling her towards the stairs. She struggled to free herself but at the top of the stairs he gave her a violent push which sent her tumbling down the stairs ending up on the hall floor. The dressing gown she was wearing fell open revealing her nakedness to the shocked onlookers. "Now fucking interview her!" screamed the manic Dennis.

A few of the guests remained after this. One advised the pressmen to leave, and another carried Diana upstairs where she just lay dazed and very shaken. Dennis was still downstairs shouting and raving. She realised she had to leave and got herself dressed in slacks and sweater, grabbed her car keys and left the house. She spent the night with friends who lived nearby. When she returned the next morning she found Dennis in tears as were some of the guests who were still at the house, and even the housekeeper. Dennis begged her forgiveness for his behaviour and even asked her to think of all the pets they owned before throwing their marriage away. Diana, of course, forgave him realising in her heart that although he was a difficult man to live with, he would be even harder to leave.

He now set out on a mission to prove how sorry he was. Property, he maintained, was the thing to invest in. The coffee bar he had was ticking along nicely and he now began to think about other business ventures.

One day he took Diana off to see an old Victorian property he had discovered on the river at Maidenhead. It was called 'Woodhurst' and it stood in several acres of grounds. With his usual great luck Dennis managed to secure the property for £12,000. His plan was to convert the house into fifteen flats, the financial implications of which frightened Diana somewhat. Dennis was very optimistic about the whole venture and set about engaging builders.

One spring evening they were both walking around the grounds and were inspired with the same idea. The swimming pool had a roof and was solid. Having climbed on to the top their thoughts turned to building a beautiful house to their own specifications above it. All thoughts of the flats were forgotten as Dennis channelled his energies into building a house fit for a film star. He finished the project in eleven weeks.

"Yield to the Night" was chosen for the Cannes Film Festival, the only British film to be selected. The festival was to be the most glittering successful week in Diana's life. Cannes proved to be everything Diana expected and she was mobbed as she walked down the Croissette on her first day there. She stayed at the luxurious Carlton hotel, was interviewed by the press, photographed leading the flower festival, and competed with a host of other performers including Susan Hayward and Doris Day for the best actress award.

"Yield to the Night" premiered on the night of 4 May and John Davis of the Rank Organisation was there to see the wonderful reception the audience gave it. At the end of the evening Diana received a standing ovation. Diana however was sure that John Davis blanked her as he left the showing, and she felt this even more when she arrived at the dinner afterwards to find there was no seat for her on the Rank table. She thought back to the time earlier in the evening before the premiere when she had stood on the balcony of her hotel looking at all the lights along the Croissette and the words she had said then came back to her "This is my night. Whatever happens in the future, no one can ever take it away."

In Britain the film was equally well received and the reviews in the serious press were some of the best of her career. "Sight and Sound" commented "Here is a British picture which is daring enough to take as its theme the last few days in the life of a murderess condemned to be hanged, and brave enough to suggest that the whole business is not one that reflects the utmost credit on society."

Sadly although the film received great praise from the critics, her usual audience stayed away, and when the film opened in London's West End on 10 September it ran for just two weeks.

The actual British premiere was another glittering affair and Police had to hold back the thousands of screaming fans as Diana arrived in a powder blue Cadillac in London's Haymarket. Diana looked down the Haymarket towards the theatre where "Remains to be Seen" had been staged. How things had moved on since this time!

After the premiere a party was held at their new home. Friends floated in the swimming pool, drank champagne and enjoyed the marvellous supper prepared by Mrs Scholl the housekeeper. Lavish parties were a regular occurrence now, mainly at the instigation of Dennis, who was never really happy unless he was entertaining multitudes of people. The new home built above the swimming pool was made to measure for parties on a grand scale with its huge stone

A tender moment from "Yield to the Night" with Michael Craig

fireplace in the drawing room. The squash court was now a private cinema with leopard skin seats, a fountain rock pool and giant framed photographs of Diana in various glamour poses. To these magnificent interiors came stars of the calibre of Rex Harrison, Dame Anna Neagle, Kim Novak and Roger Moore, along with producers and directors such as Otto Preminger and John Houston.

Dennis always chose the guests, especially the male ones as, to quote Diana herself, "he was increasingly paranoiac about any man taking away his 'shiny doll' which was what he affectionately called me."

Sadly the success of "Yield to the Night" did not bring Diana any further work apart from a Bob Hope NBC television spectacular that had been filmed in England. The only film the Rank Organisation had offered was a Norman Wisdom comedy which was hardly a fitting follow up to her great dramatic performance in "Yield", and Dennis dismissed the offer as "rubbish".

It was a mystery why British film producers could not find another vehicle for her talent. It was almost as if they were frightened of this new dramatic Diana Dors, and did not know what to do with her. Then suddenly Hollywood wanted her. The Bob Hope show had been screened in the USA and showed a British blonde who appeared to have imitated Marilyn Monroe and was a great double act with Bob.

Diana on a fashion magazine shoot in London (1956)

12

Welcome To Hollywood

RKO Films which had once been controlled by Howard Hughes, but was at this time financed by General Teleradio, offered her $85,000 to appear in a film called 'I Married A Woman' with a comedian called George Gobel. Gobel was a big comedy star in the USA, but as yet had not been seen in England. RKO thoughts were that Diana would help sell him to British audiences, and he would help sell her to American audiences.

At last that childhood dream of becoming a Hollywood film star was becoming a reality. Ironically the departure of Diana for America coincided with the arrival of Marilyn Monroe from America as she was coming to Britain to star with Sir Laurence Olivier in a film version of the stage play 'The Sleeping Prince' which was to be titled 'The Prince and The Showgirl'.

Marilyn Monroe was five years older than Diana but there were many parallels in their stories. As was Diana, Marilyn had been discovered by a forces photographer, and her pin up portraits had brought her to the attention of a Hollywood studio. Also like Diana she went under contract to a studio – 20th Century Fox in 1946. She was also a bottle blonde, attended a 'charm school', and changed her name.

However, as Diana pointed out many times, Marilyn's career did not really take off until 1950 when she made 'The Asphalt Jungle', and she did not receive top billing until 1953 with the release of

'Niagara' in which she co-starred with William Holden. As far as Diana was concerned Marilyn was a latecomer whose body of work had encompassed far less fields than her own. She did not know it at the time, but she would never escape being 'Britain's answer to Marilyn Monroe'. If things had been different in the United Kingdom and our film industry had been as big as that in America it may have been a totally different story.

Marilyn's arrival in Britain was scheduled for 14 July 1956, a few days before Diana began work on her Hollywood debut. One of her representatives contacted Diana about renting the Penthouse to her while she was filming. When he inspected it he was delighted because of its luxury, and felt it was perfect for a star of her magnitude. However because of Marilyn's shyness and need for privacy the tenancy never became a reality, as the property was already a tourist attraction for the many who took boat trips down the Thames. This was the version that Diana told, but Damon Wise in his biography tells it slightly differently "In actual fact, he had already decided it was 'much too small' for Monroe's purposes and perhaps more importantly had 'no class at all'" Whichever version is the true one mattered little to Diana as she had her Hollywood dream about to be realised.

Because Dennis had a fear of flying it was arranged that they sailed to New York from Southampton, but on arrival they would have to fly on to Los Angeles. A lavish farewell party was held on the ship in the state suite where many friends and colleagues wished her bon voyage. Diana, although naturally thrilled at the prospect of her contract with RKO was nonetheless apprehensive at visiting new territory and the loneliness she would feel being so far from everything familiar.

The journey took five days, then the big day arrived and as they approached New York harbour they saw for the first time the Manhattan skyline and the Statue of Liberty. A few hours before the ship docked reporters arrived in a coastguard boat to interview her. Diana arrived in the ship's lounge in a knee length white dress with a criss cross single strap which emphasised her curves and cleavage to perfection. Diana commented "Isn't this wonderful. We all speak the same language". A passing porter quipped "Lady you don't need no language".

Diana and Dennis had been booked into the Sherry Netherland Hotel on Fifth Avenue and an air conditioned Cadillac had been provided for the journey there. After just an hour to change and rest, Diana was taken to the exclusive 21 Club for a cocktail reception and lunch. After lunch she moved from table to table talking to various reporters. Naturally comparisons began between her and Monroe:

Q. It's ironic that you should arrive in America just as Marilyn Monroe is heading for London.
A. Yes its lend-lease.
Q. Have you met Marilyn?
A. No, but I'd certainly like to.
Q. What do you think of the comparisons that are being made?
A. I don't mind. I'm 36.5-24-35. I don't know how that compares with Marilyn, but if you men don't know, does it matter? If I must be compared with someone, it's not bad company.

RKO assigned a barrage of public relations men to look after her. Limousines were always at her disposal, and tickets were available for every Broadway show including 'My Fair Lady' which was the hit of the decade. Despite her confident answers to the press, the comparisons with Marilyn did unnerve Diana. All the work she had done – the Bob Hope Special excepted – meant nothing to the Americans. They had not seen 'Yield to the Night', the films, plays and variety work she had appeared in were unknown to them. However the newspaper coverage she received was fantastic on both sides of the atlantic. Headlines such as 'Britain's Dynamite Explodes on the City' (New York Post) and 'A Fascinating Fabrication of Femininity' (New York Mirror) made her feel that perhaps all would be well.

After a few days in New York they flew on to Los Angeles. More press were there to greet them and the head of RKO – William Dozier. They had been booked in to the exclusive Beverly Hills Hotel where another press reception was held. Heading this particular breed were the two famous heads of the film columnist world - Louella Parsons and Hedda Hopper. They both had great power and everyone was terrified of them. Louella Parsons had strong catholic beliefs but one would hardly have thought of her as Christian with the amount of vitriol she put into her columns. Hedda Hopper was a former film actress who had strong fascist political views.

Dennis was to get off to a bad start with her as he turned on his usual charm to no effect. When he expressed the view that he could not believe this lovely lady could deserve the reputation of being unkind to anyone the icy retort came back "okay Hamilton don't overdo it". This came as a complete shock to Dennis. Having been able to handle the British press with ease, this new type of hard nosed columnist was something he had never encountered before, and Diana commented that it was something he never got used to.

Diana, on the other hand, was doing extremely well with the American press and her worries about being away from familiar territory began to lessen. She was quoted as saying "I have no studio obligations back home, and if I like the pictures and the roles here I may stay on. I made it to Hollywood on my own terms. I was planning to come here eventually. I am on time".

William Dozier announced that he had had to use all his powers of persuasion with Diana to get her to sign a long term contract. His original plan to get her to agree to a seven year contract had gradually diminished, first to three years, then to two films, and then to one. He announced however that he had two more ideas for Diana's consideration and if they appealed to her, they were definite engagements.

Preparations were now underway for 'I Married a Woman' and Diana was taken to the RKO studios to meet all the production staff and have make up and dress tests. She was overwhelmed at the care and attention to detail which they all took at the American studios. It made the English approach to films seem very amateurish indeed.

Shortly after filming began, and knowing how RKO wanted her to sign to a long term contract, they began talking again with Dozier. He offered her a three year contract for one picture a year, but with influence from Dennis she held out for five. Finally a three year no option agreement was signed. Telling the press it was worth £50,000 per picture she went on to say "It's only in America I can get more money, better parts and a world- wide build up".

"I Married A Woman" with George Gobel

Dennis found them a property to rent; a Spanish style villa just off Sunset Boulevard, the previous tenant had been Marlene Dietrich. Problems began to arise because he had nothing to do. All his property and business interests were at home, so while Diana was at the studios all he had to do was manage the domestic scene. He was losing his strangle hold over her even more now, and the way he always referred to her as "Dors" was not liked by the Americans who rightfully felt it showed a lack of respect.

One classic example of this was an evening when they were in the company of William Dozier and his wife Ann Rutherford. During the course of the conversation it came to light that Diana had no mink coat. She told them both that Dennis did not like the idea of her in one. The retort from Dennis "Dors looks dreadful in a fur coat" made them both wince. When Diana arrived at the studios next day she was summoned to Bill Dozier's office where lying on the sofa were three beautiful mink stoles. Diana chose a silver blue one. Dennis froze when he saw it later but for once said nothing. He just did not seem capable of understanding that men could do nice things for women without any sexual motives.

Having now agreed a contract with RKO Dennis decided it was time to buy a property in America. This was something Diana was not happy about as she liked the rented accommodation they were in, and also felt that with the Rank contract and all their business interests in England it was going to be rather a waste of money, but as usual Dennis got the final say. By August he had found the home he wanted 'Hillside House' which was in the Coldwater Canyon area. It was reputed to have cost £62,500 and the studio loaned him the money to buy it on the strength of Diana's contract. The house was indeed luxurious, but what they both soon realised was that the extravagant lifestyle which so impressed back in Britain made no impression in Hollywood where this type of lifestyle was commonplace. As Diana was to comment in 1981 "Buying a fabulous home with all the trimmings achieved nothing for us and was simply a waste of money".

Publicity portrait from "I Married A Woman"

13

The Hollywood Party And Shattered Dreams

The Hamiltons, or rather Dennis, wanted to show off their house and began preparations for a lavish party. Diana's society hairdresser friend Raymond "Teasy-Weasy" Bessone was very interested to hear of the large sums of money that Diana was able to command in the USA. Big publicity was generated to the press that he was coming over to America, and was going to create a new hairstyle for her, for which she was going to pay him $5,000. The press lapped it up, while Dennis made preparations for the party at which Raymond would be guest of honour, and thereby be launched in Hollywood. Diana continued to work at the studios, Bob Hope was filming at Columbia Studios which were next door and so she came into contact with him frequently. Bob's agent Louis Shurr was now representing Diana in America, and plans were afoot for her to star with Bob in some remakes of old Jean Harlow films 'Blonde Bombshell' and 'Platinum Blonde'.

The press continued to compare her with Monroe, and when an offer came from 20th Century Fox for her to star with Marilyn's former co-star Tom Ewell in a follow up to 'The Seven Year Itch', Dennis turned it down for her saying that the press would make comparisons even more if she took it, much to Diana's regret as 'The Girl Can't Help It', which was the release title of the film, turned out to be the best film Jayne Mansfield ever made.

Diana found she was now becoming homesick for England. The

first weeks with so much going on had been exhilarating, and the things she had dreamed about when reading the film magazines were becoming a reality. The glamour, the sunshine, and the high standard of living began to make her wish for the softer charms and slower pace of life in England. She had achieved her ultimate ambition to go to Hollywood, and now the dream was realised, panic set in. Where did she go from here? She little realised that the pinnacle she had reached was to be very short lived, and that the arrival of Raymond would be the beginning of the death knell of her Hollywood career.

Diana's actor friend Peter Reynolds, who had appeared with her in 'The Last Page', arrived in the states a few weeks ahead of Raymond. Having read the wonderful stories of Diana's treatment in the country, he decided he would try his luck, and so began the round of visiting casting directors and agents.

Raymond duly arrived and the lavish party was arranged for 19 August 1956. Invitations were sent out to some of the biggest names in the film industry including Lana Turner, Greer Garson, Doris Day, Debbie Reynolds, Eddie Fisher and Zsa Zsa Gabor. The invitations read "We would be delighted if you could come to a ding-dong in honour of the arrival in Hollywood of our good friend Raymond". When asked what the term "ding-dong" meant, Dennis replied that it was a cocktail party that "could develop". How true this would turn out to be!

On the night 250 guests arrived at the Hamilton's residence. Raymond's name arranged in flowers floated on top of the swimming pool. Ten waiters were hired and the catering was sumptuous. As the party was to be informal, Diana decided not to wear one of her glamorous dresses. Instead she wore blue slacks with a matching blouse, wide leather belt, diamante studded high heeled sandals and the diamond wrist watch that was Dennis' first wedding anniversary present to her.

The party progressed well and guests were assembling near to the swimming pool. Dennis and Diana were talking to Diana's agent Louis Shurr and dress designer Howard Shoup. Suddenly someone gave Diana a push. She put out her arms but there was nothing to hold on to, and she and the three men all toppled backwards into the pool. Luckily for all concerned it was the shallow end otherwise the outcome might have been rather different. Dennis climbed out of the pool in a fury "Who did it? Who did it? I'll give $5,000 to anybody who tells me!"

The pair of legs he saw disappearing through the crowd belonged to thirty-two year old United Press Photographer Stewart Sawyer. Without waiting for any explanations, Dennis knocked him to the ground, kicking him and screaming abuse "Any man who comes to my house, eats my food, drinks my liquor, then throws me in my own fucking pool, deserves everything he gets!"

The guests were shocked to see this violent confrontation. As the Los Angeles Police arrived Dennis was still in full flow boasting that he had once been a boxer. Stars not wanting bad publicity quickly left, and the next day Diana and Dennis found themselves crucified in the press, What had originally been intended as a sophisticated party was now described as a "drunken orgy hosted by two English publicity seeking degenerates". The biggest headline read "Go Home Diana and take Mr Dors with You".

Doctors gave their verdict on the extent of the injuries incurred – Diana had bruises and abrasions on her arms and a possible sprained back. Dennis had grazed and swollen knuckles. Stewart Sawyer came off worst having suffered cuts and bruises on his face head and ribs, and a suspected broken nose. Sawyer posed with his injuries for publicity photographs. No one would believe that the press hungry Hamiltons had not staged the whole event to get world wide publicity which is of course what they got.

Sawyer initially denied Dennis' accusations but his story gradually changed since he was to say "I didn't do it deliberately. I may have bumped against them. All I remember is lying on the ground and someone hitting me. Then I passed out. Sure, I had a couple of drinks, like everyone else …" Sawyer's wife retaliated by saying "Just wait till I get my hands on that Diana Dors, I'll kick her where it hurts most".

The National Enquirer ran a 3,000 word piece by Lewis Onslow that said "America has two imports she can do without. They are a bizarre, boisterous couple who have thrived on publicity – good and bad – and whose zany, riotous exploits have reverberated on both sides of the Atlantic … Miss Dors is Britain's answer to Marilyn Monroe.

Dennis Hamilton is her lusty husband – and nobody's answer to anything".

With regard to the swimming pool incident at the party he went on to say "Some people may have found it amusing. We do not agree. The exhibition was sheer bad manners. Inexcusable bad manners – even if the whole thing was a publicity stunt….We have enough bizarre characters in this country without importing others who have no regard for the common standard of decent behaviour".

The heads of RKO became very worried about all the adverse publicity. The Hollywood Reporter said "Up the Hammer and Sickle girl, and gather those Yankee dollars while you may". Following a meeting with Bill Dozier, she was instructed to telephone all the columnists and apologise, and agreeing that Dennis had been wrong to take the law into his own hands. RKO were also looking into Diana's contract to see if they had grounds to fire her, but the whole incident was not a clear cut issue. For one thing Diana continued to declare her innocence, and for another the film company knew it would be difficult to uphold in a court of law the sacking of an actress because of her husband's behaviour.

In any case plans were already in hand for her next film "The Lady and the Prowler" (it would be released as "The Unholy Wife"). Originally her co-star on this production was to have been Ernest Borgnine, but he was unavailable so the role was taken on by Rod Steiger – a strong stage actor with a string of intense screen roles to his name. Following naval service during the Second World War, he used a scholarship from the Government's GI Bill programme to study acting, which finally took him to the Actors Studio, a workshop founded in New York in 1947. When Lee Strasberg took over at the helm two years later he developed a new approach to acting which was known as 'The Method', and was the approach Steiger used in his work. Diana was bowled over by his talent, and said in later years that he was the best actor she had ever worked with.

The film was a drama set in the wine-growing area of northern California, and directed by John Farrow, father of actress Mia Farrow. Known in the industry as 'Fearless Farrow', he came with a somewhat formidable reputation but Diana struck up an instant rapport with him, due to her total professionalism with which he was very impressed. He even had a guitarist engaged to serenade her between takes. Filming went well, but Bill Dozier was getting increasingly worried due to the bad press Diana was still receiving. Things were not helped when she found herself falling in love with her co-star Rod Steiger.

Diana undergoing make up and hair checks on the set of "The Unholy Wife"

14

The Unholy Wife

Dennis was unaware of the danger as he had his eye on handsome American actor Tom Tryon who was playing Diana's cowboy lover in the film. In Dennis' mind, he was exactly the type of man Diana would fall for, but he was wrong. After five years of being under his thumb, she craved a man whom she could both love and respect. Rod Steiger to her mind fulfilled that requirement. Unlike Dennis he was not crude and surly in his treatment towards her and out for what he could get, treating her as a commodity. Rod made her feel like a real woman.

Steiger inspired her with his acting talent, and gave a new impetus to her own acting skills. Suddenly she found her acting ambitions renewed and having to draw on all her own reserves to match his acting talents. As is often the case when a woman falls in love with someone else, it is difficult to keep the feelings hidden and this is what happened to Diana when at home with Dennis. As the affair grew stronger she revealed the facts to Dennis and as can be imagined he went completely mad and arrived that same week at the RKO studios in search of Steiger and according to Diana in her autobiography, he had a shotgun as well.

Diana was summoned to Bill Dozier's office where she was warned about the folly of her behaviour. He warned her that if the press got hold of the story they would crucify them both, as would 'The Woman's Catholic Guild'. After the bad publicity following the swimming pool affair he could not guarantee that RKO wouldn't pull the 'morals clause' and cancel her contract. In Dozier's mind it was purely just a sexual affair but to Diana it was far more than that.

Dennis now took some action which he thought would bring Diana down to earth. He announced that he was flying back to England. In his mind he thought Diana would not be able to manage without him and it would bring her to her senses, but he was wrong. His departure to her mind made it possible for her to carry on the affair without any hindrance from him. To keep the gossip columnists at bay it was announced that Dennis had to go home to England on business. Diana stayed at Rod's house above Laurel Canyon and so infatuated with one another were they, that they threw caution to the wind and began driving to the studios together, which soon became noted by the press.

In England, Dennis was advising the press that things were alright, but because of Diana's lack of discretion, the story came out. The consequences of this were that Dennis and his business associate Jimmy Melon flew to Hollywood to try and cover up the scandal. Diana found herself miserable and desolate as the press stuck their knives in. Steiger went to a hideaway in Malibu Beach, leaving her alone to face Dennis on his arrival. Over the next week he did all in his power to win her affections back but all the gifts in the world could not erase the plain fact – that her marriage was a sham. In her mind she knew that the Steiger affair was doomed, but something made her believe that they could win through.

Bill Dozier made it clear to Diana that she and Dennis had to convince the press that they were still together. The director of 'The Unholy Wife' used his influence with Louella Parsons to patch over the cracks, and this resulted in Diana and Dennis having to visit her and ask for forgiveness with a rehearsed speech by Diana "And I'm sorry I lied Louella, but I was foolish to fall in love with Rod Steiger and only tried to save my marriage by covering up the problems Dennis and I were having. As you can see we are now happily reconciled and we both beg your forgiveness". Forgiveness was duly granted by Louella to her and to Dennis, and both parties thought that was the end of the matter, not so for Diana as she was still deeply in love with Steiger.

The atmosphere at home and at work became hard to bear. At the studios and on the set Diana and Steiger had to be very cautious, never daring to exchange too much for fear of further rumours. In the end Dennis returned to England with Jimmy Mellon. The British press made a great deal of the whole business, helped enormously by Dennis who gave a press statement at the airport relating the full facts of the Steiger affair and ending with the sad words "Diana is not the little girl I knew anymore". In partial revenge for what Diana had done, he set out on a course to destroy other people's marriages. One of his first conquests was Raymond's wife Jennifer, and a steady affair began with young starlet Shirley Anne Field, who was getting a lot of publicity at the time, and Dennis had the idea that he could turn her into another Diana Dors.

Meanwhile the affair between Steiger and Diana continued. They had to be extremely discreet, and whenever possible Diana went out to his beach house at Malibu which was an idyllic setting for romance. Rod wrote poetry to which she listened attentively and enthralled. As she herself said in 1981 "When a woman is in love, she cannot see further than the face of the man she adores, and all the time Rod and I enjoyed each other at Malibu I had no interest in the direction my life was taking". The end of the romance was just around the corner. Rod flew to New York where his wife was acting in a Broadway play, to sort out his marital problems. Diana stayed on in Malibu and while there she received a telephone call from Rod "You must go home for a while" he said, and then continued "I'm confused, we're both confused. Live your life and enjoy it".

Any kind of life for Diana without him had not entered her mind, and the bottom just dropped out of her world. As an actress Hollywood was dead for her. Because of all the bad publicity she had received, there were no plans for another film for her, and so on a bleak November day in 1956 she returned to England taking a suite at the Dorchester Hotel in Park Lane on arrival. The low spirits she was now experiencing are best summed up in her own words. "I had been away for five months, had earnt something in the region of half a million dollars and had lost it, along with a career, a Hollywood mansion, a husband and a lover. What lay ahead of me now?"

On the set of "The Unholy Wife" with Director John Farrow

The return from America with husband Dennis 14 November 1956

Mr Hamilton however was planning a careful strategy to win her back. First of all he contacted the press and then he sent a limousine to the Dorchester to take her to the Penthouse to have as he put it "a quiet talk". This actually lasted over thirty six hours and at the end of this Dennis announced to the press that they had agreed on a reconciliation, and Diana was once more caught in the spider's web, basically because there was nothing else. After so much upset in their marriage, it was of course inevitable that there would be scars, and Dennis happily continued with most of the affairs he had begun during the split, and people now began to relate to Diana stories of his exploits with various women. She felt unable to retaliate because of her own affair with Steiger which Dennis used as a weapon against her saying that she was the one who had upset the marriage.

With the end of 1956 in sight and the arrival of Christmas, the Penthouse was full of his friends at a lavish party, all of whom delighted in telling Diana what a wonderful man he was. This contrasts rather sharply with the story Diana related of when his mother called them to wish them both a Happy Christmas. He called her a liar and a nymphomaniac. His actual behaviour was becoming more and more erratic now, and the brainstorms he had experienced in past years were becoming more and more frequent. Something said in all innocence could trigger off a violent reaction. A few days after the Christmas party Dennis was involved in a fight in Maidstone High Street with a car driver who refused to pull over and let him overtake. He actually stopped the thirty eight year old motorist and punched him in the face. Luckily for Dennis the case never got to court, as a settlement was reached and the charges were dropped.

The advent of 1957 saw neither of Diana's films for RKO released, and in consequence of all the adverse publicity she had received, they had no plans to use her in any forthcoming projects. January however did see the American release of 'Yield to the Night' to good reviews. The New York Times said "The extremely trim Miss Dors, in case anybody wonders or cares, *can* act" and later in the review went on to say "Her restrained haggard transition from listless empathy to numb terror is a pip in a shattering, haunting and generally sterling little picture".

15

Back In The English Studios

Diana's next film 'The Long Haul' was due to start filming in February 1957, her co-star Robert Mitchum. Prior to this she and Dennis took a holiday in Malaga with old actress friend Sandra Dorne and her husband Patrick Holt who had appeared with Diana in 'Miss Tulip Stays the Night'. On return from the holiday they discovered that Mitchum had dropped out and had been replaced by the ruggedly handsome Victor Mature. Dennis was extremely worried by this change of casting as Mature had a notorious reputation as a womanizer but as things panned out he should have been worried by an entirely different man.

Diana was offered a fee of £20,000 for the film, but £10,000 of this was to be paid in cash as a 'tax fiddle'. An uncle of Diana's was enlisted to help. This involved him in collecting the money in a suitcase from the producer's office, taking his own cut and passing the rest on to Dennis. The director of 'The Long Haul' – Ken Hughes – was an old friend of the Hamilton's, and one evening appeared at their home with a young starlet who was his latest girlfriend. During the course of the evening she and Diana became more chatty and the topic of conversation turned to Rod Steiger. It turned out that not only had the young woman had an affair with him, but that the same romantic poetry he had quoted to Diana, he had also quoted to her. She immediately realised that Steiger was just the same as every other actor she had met and he suddenly fell from the pedestal on which she had placed him.

To return to the film and the threat posed by Victor Mature. Diana certainly found him amusing, but after working with a man of Steiger's acting calibre there was no way she could have fallen for him. Steiger was a deeply complex man, whereas Mature was your typical Hollywood hunk. An extremely attractive man, but well aware that he would not win any great accolades for his acting ability. He was always fearful of losing his good looks which had won him so many leading roles, and doubles were always engaged for any complex stunts involved in his films. On 'The Long Haul' it was a handsome young man called Tommy Yeardye who filled this role and it was he who Diana became attracted to.

It began as a studio fling. Diana was a lonely woman trapped in a marriage she did not want to be in. Yeardye was courteous and polite, and treated her with both respect and admiration. She gradually found herself enjoying his company more and more with each day that passed and gradually began to have an affair with him. It was Dennis' predilection for eavesdropping that brought the affair to his attention. Comedian Jon Pertwee was staying at their home for the weekend along with his first wife – actress Jean Marsh. Jon was performing in cabaret in Croydon, and Dennis announced that he was popping out but would be back as it was about an hour till dinner. The two girls were talking and Jon's wife mentioned an actor with whom she had fallen in love, and Diana went on to tell her about the handsome young stuntman she had fallen for on 'The Long Haul'. Dennis returned along with some more friends, and "Sholly" the housekeeper announced that dinner was ready. Dennis urged them all into the dining room and said he would join them. Ten minutes later a terrible crash came from the drawing room. Diana rushed out to find he had smashed a large glass table and was continuing to smash various ornaments. She was soon to find out the reason for his tirade. Just before he had left the house he had switched on a hidden tape recorder and had just listened to the results of his work. The plan had been to confront Jean about her love affair, but the plan had gone wrong as he heard far more than he had bargained for. The result of his fury was that the two women fled from the house and Diana drove them both back to London.

"The Long Haul" with Victor Mature

However, with 'The Long Haul' still to complete, a compromise had to be reached and Diana once more found herself returning to Dennis. His ten per cent as her manager was dependent on her completing the film, and he also knew that the BBC were planning to have her as a subject for their 'This is your Life' programme. 'The Long Haul' was now entering a phase of having to shoot night scenes. Before Diana was due at the studios one night for filming, Dennis suggested that they go to a show. Diana found herself at a theatre where she was to be the star of the evening as the cameras turned on her for the Eamonn Andrews programme 'This is your Life'. The evening was a nostalgic and emotional one for her with the appearance of her father, Auntie Kit, other family members, and her old elocution teacher. The big surprise of the evening was not such a pleasant one for Diana however as the photographer who had pushed them into the swimming pool – Stewart Sawyer, had been flown in from Hollywood "I've come 6,000 miles to shake you hand" said Sawyer. "If I'd known you were coming I'd have worn my swimsuit" was Diana's reply.

As far as Diana was concerned the marriage was now over and the sham of happiness she and Dennis presented to the world was purely for business reasons. As far as Dennis was concerned, Diana was his investment, without her he would have no income, but he was clever enough to make her believe that without him she would be incapable of managing her finances. It really was a case of burying their differences for business reasons. Dennis was protecting his investment, Diana wanted to keep her public profile high, and as divorce was still frowned upon in Britain it was best to keep the status quo.

The situation during the following weeks did not improve and then most unexpectedly Dennis announced that he was leaving her. Diana was not convinced in her mind that he meant it, but on her return from the studios he had indeed gone taking his belongings with him. Sholly the housekeeper had remained, but as Diana later said "I didn't know she'd been left there purposely to spy!" Diana experienced a great feeling of freedom, and invited Tommy and some of his friends down for a party. It was the first time he had visited the Penthouse. On the Sunday Diana went out for a drive with Tommy, accompanied by John Hoey, a bubble-gum-machine tycoon, and actress Shani Wallis who was later to play Nancy in the film of the musical 'Oliver'. On their return, Sholly emerged to say that Dennis had called and wanted to see her. According to Diana she was told "It's all right, Mr Hamilton's not in a temper, he just wants you to come in and sign some papers." However, Diana did not find this to be the case. Dennis, realising that he had lost Diana and his 'meal ticket', was safeguarding his interests. When Diana entered he burst in on her with a shotgun. Pointing it at her he backed her into the nearest room, entering himself and locking the door behind him. He then proceeded to smash the window with the barrel of the shotgun pointing at the three in the car and telling them to "get going".

A piece of paper was then thrown at Diana with the command that she was to sign it. This was a list compiled by Dennis of all the men she was supposed to have had an affair with during their marriage, some of which she had only met professionally in passing. Another piece of paper listed all the items she was to sign over to him, this included virtually all the properties, apart from the Penthouse, and the Cadillac which he had given her as a present, plus all the money in the bank. Diana nervously signed both pieces of paper and moved towards the door, but Dennis in his uncontrollable anger punched her in the head, and she sank to the floor dazed and with a terrible pain in the side of her head.

Tommy meanwhile fearful for Diana's safety after the shotgun had appeared rushed to the house. The front door was locked but he pushed his fist through the glass panel and opened it from the inside. Bursting into the room he flung himself at Hamilton and they grappled to the floor. Tommy being so much stronger soon overpowered Dennis and had him laid out on the floor. As he helped her from the room she heard Dennis sob "Dors how could you do this to me. I loved you so much".

This was the final scene, and the curtain came down on their marriage. Tommy took her to stay at his parent's home in London and also to see a Doctor who told her she had a punctured eardrum from the blow. Staying with Tommy's parents proved impractical, mainly because of her huge wardrobe of clothes, but she found a temporary solution to the problem as a film director friend rented her his mews home in Belgravia for a month.

When 'The Long Haul' was completed, Dennis sent her just £1,000 of the £20,000 she had earned. Something had to be done about the situation as Diana would have to leave Belgravia and find somewhere else to live. Legal advice was sought and although the statements she signed had been "under duress", it was still decided that Dennis was to have all the properties except the Penthouse. The stipulation was that she should live there without harassment from her husband. To ensure this was adhered to, Tommy moved back with her to act as bodyguard. Because of the way Dennis had cheated her out of so much money on 'The Long Haul' she made sure that on her next film she would get her full fee.

Diana with Tommy Yeardye holidaying
on the French Riviera

Act Two

16

An International Film And Farewell To Tommy

Many British actors were being approached by continental film producers at this time, and some such as Belinda Lee were soon to establish themselves with new European careers. Director Vittorio Gassman wanted Diana for a film called 'The Girl Who Rode in the Palio'. Her salary was to be $85,000 and had been negotiated by Dennis before the split. The story concerned a girl who wins a trip to Sienna in a competition and then falls in love with an Italian prince. While they were filming in Rome she arranged for Tommy's parents to join them for a holiday and then they went on to Florence, which Diana described as "a beautiful city filled with statues of god-like men, all of whom Tommy, with his muscle-building ideals admired a great deal."

The final shots of the film were done in Sienna, where a famous horse race, the Palio, had been run for a thousand years. It was a violent event with riders lashing each other with bull whips as they competed for the honour and glory of winning. Before the race commenced the competitors would take their horses into church and pray, which struck everyone as rather funny, but what made it even more amusing to Diana was that the American girl she was playing was supposed to win the race!

The filming days were long and arduous, but Diana enjoyed the experience, although she was beginning to have doubts about her future with Tommy which even the hot Italian nights could not dispel.

"The Girl Who Rode in the Palio" with Vittorio Gassman

He had been a rock throughout the problems with Dennis, but he was just too keen to stay in the background. Since moving in with Diana he had not worked very much, and she needed a man with style, panache, and exciting plans – somebody like Dennis.

They returned to England with Diana still owed money for the film and even with lengthy legal battles she was not to get it all. She found herself in quite a difficult predicament now she was back in the Penthouse, as Dennis was living just next door in 'Woodhurst'. He would occasionally phone her or pop round on some pretext in order to ingratiate himself with her but to quote Diana "for the rest of the time, car loads of girls were being driven in and out at all times of the day or night."

One day when Tommy was away in London he invited her round to see all the improvements he had made on "Woodhurst". Proudly he displayed antiques he had purchased as they drank wine from crystal goblets. There was a grand piano, which he could not play, in the corner, and the shelves around the room were full of leather bound books. He presented a volume to her which was a collection of poems by Rupert Brooke, who was his favourite poet. As she left he said "no one will ever love you the way I did." When she got back she opened the book and read the inscription inside "To my darling wife. I love you more today than yesterday, and less than tomorrow." There were also indications of poems she should read. The shortest one touched her most.

The way of Love was thus,
He was born, one winter morn,
With hands delicious,
And it was well with us.
Love came our quiet way,
Lit pride in us, and died in us,
All in a winter's day.
There is no more to say.

This was the other side of Dennis Hamilton, the gentle loving man. Could she try again with him? Deep down inside she knew the answer was no.

The Rank Organisation was not pleased with all the adverse publicity she had been receiving. Her two Hollywood films had not been a success, and then there had been the swimming pool incident, the reconciliation and then the second break up from Dennis, and finally the dreadful reviews for 'The Long Haul'. All this contributed to the downward spiral of her career. There was little happening on the work front for her in Britain. In America 'The Unholy Wife' had yet to be released, and the thought of moving back to Hollywood did not fire her with enthusiasm. Even if she did go back she knew it would not be permanent due to the pressure of the media there "It's too easy to end up slashing your wrists in the bathroom or drinking yourself to sleep." She did make a short trip to the States for an appearance on 'The Perry Como Show', and on her return received the welcome news that director Gordon Parry wanted her for the female lead role in his latest film 'Tread Softly Stranger" at a fee of £20,000.

Filming took place at Walton Studios in Surrey and on location in Rotherham, South Yorkshire. Set in the industrial North, Diana's character 'Calico' worked as a hostess in a club. Her leading man was played by handsome George Baker who in later life would fame for his television portrayal of Chief Inspector Wexford in "The Ruth Rendell Mysteries"

The story based on a play by the Yorkshire playwright Jack Popplewell centres on two brothers Johnny (George Baker) and Dave (Terence Morgan) in love with the same girl 'Calico'. Dave has been taking money from the factory where he works as a wages clerk to buy expensive gifts for her. The auditors are coming to the factory in a few days to balance the books and he is naturally in a panic. Johnny is convinced that he can win the money Dave needs by backing a horse, but while Johnny is at the races, Calico persuades him to break into the factory and take the wages that are left in the safe overnight. The robbery goes wrong and he shoots the night watchman.

In 2002 I had the pleasure of meeting George Baker at a theatre function where he spoke to me fondly of Diana. Their paths had crossed several times before they worked together. "She always looked unbelievably glamorous."

"Tread Softly Stranger" with George Baker

"Tread Softly Stranger" with George Baker

In his autobiography he recalls the film

"-I was filming on location in Sheffield with *Tread Softly Stranger*. We were working in Steel, Peach and Tozer's steel works – there was still a steel industry in England in those days. It was a good film, with a wonderful performance by Wilfrid Lawson. Also in the cast was Di Dors: although I'd known her for several years, *Tread Softly Stranger* was the first time we'd worked together. She was a no-nonsense professional and I already knew she had a smashing sense of humour."

She was offered another film 'Passport to Shame'. Not the lead but a support role at a fee of £8,000 which was far below her usual rate. French actress Odile Versois took the lead in a story about a French girl who is tricked into coming to England as a companion but is going to be forced into prostitution. Brenda de Banzie and Herbert Lom played the villains running the prostitution racket, with Eddie Constantine as a taxi driver and Diana as a prostitute trying to rescue her.

During the filming of 'Passport to Shame' she was contacted by variety agent Joe Collins asking if she would be interested in taking the 'Diana Dors Show' around more variety theatres and cinemas. Joe said he could fill the bill with top notch variety acts but that they would need a good comedian to link everything together. Diana could not think of anyone apart from an actor friend Digby Wolfe who was making a splash as a television comedian, but Tommy Yeardye suggested a young comedian they had recently seen at the Stork Club in London – Richard (Dickie) Dawson.

While filming additional shots for 'Passport to Shame,' Dickie would visit the set and together he and Diana wrote a script for the show. She found him both amusing and quick witted and was pleased that Tommy had suggested him. The tour commenced in Coventry and was a great success. Diana found Dickie easy to work with and as the weeks went on she found she was enjoying his company both on and off stage more and more, and gradually enjoyment turned to love. After the domineering relationship she had had with Dennis, she was relieved to find someone who did not want to mould her. However, some of Diana's friends did not believe him to be sincere and felt that he was just using her to further his own career.

"Passport to Shame" as "Vicki

Her romance continued to blossom and she told Tommy how she was feeling about Dickie. Whilst the tour continued Tommy remained in the farmhouse she had brought at Billingshurt. When the tour ended she contacted him and asked him to leave so that the place would be empty for her return along with Dickie. After a hard exchange of words he concluded by telling her he had done something she would not like. To avoid Dennis getting hold of any of her money, Diana had placed £12,000 in a safe deposit box at Harrods to which Tommy also had access. When she went to Harrods and called for her box she discovered that he had removed every penny of the money. She contacted his mother to ascertain his whereabouts but she refused to offer any information and hotly denied that her son could have done such a thing. Diana got the same reaction from all their mutual friends, and in the end she reported the incident at Chelsea Police Station. They promised to do what they could to help but nothing happened until a friend rang Diana to say that his wife, who was on holiday in the South of France, had seen Tommy lying on the beach at Cannes where he was staying at the same hotel as herself. Diana's friend Frank Craddock immediately informed the French Police who insisted Tommy return to England at once to give his account of the matter.

The newspapers were now full of the incident and Diana began to worry as the taxman would clearly be interested in the £12,000. Photographs appeared of Tommy's arrival at London Airport and reports circulated in which he said he had taken the money in order to teach her a lesson. The outcome was that he had hidden the money in a safe place until she had come to her senses. For her part Diana did not want to press charges against a man to whom for over a year she had been so close. "You're a fool to fall in love with Dawson" Tommy said bitterly "He'll turn out to be like all the rest of the men in your life." Diana was reunited with her money at her solicitor's office in Holborn. Yeardye went on to do very well for himself with various business projects, eventually moving to the west coast of America as business manager for Vidal Sassoon.

17

Goodbye Dennis

At the beginning of October 1958 Dennis was admitted to the London clinic supposedly suffering from serious heart trouble. When the news reached Diana she was on tour and playing to two houses every night. When she called the hospital she was asked not to visit, so she sent him some roses. At around the same time she herself began to develop health problems as acute stomach pains kept recurring which caused her to double over in agony. It was so bad at one point that a doctor had to be called in the middle of the night to administer morphine. The doctor diagnosed pancreatitis. Diana had been performing at the Finsbury Park Empire when she collapsed. Dickie cared for her, sometimes lavishing her with expensive presents. Diana was so in love with him that she never stopped to consider where the money was coming from to pay for these. She just enjoyed his attentiveness.

When recovered, she visited Dennis in the hospital where, to use her own words, she found him in a "highly emotional state." He explained to her that he had a heart infection and that he was receiving twenty injections a day. Up until his admittance to hospital he had been living with blonde actress Vera Day. She explained to Diana how negative he was being about everything and how he kept insisting that he was going to die. Diana pointed out that Dennis had always enjoyed good health and was probably just not coping very well with being confined in hospital.

In December Diana accepted a cabaret engagement in Johannesburg which earned her £1,000. She had also received, through an American agent she knew, a contract to appear on the Steve Allen television show in New York. The fee was $7,000 and a flight to New York was arranged for her and Dickie on 3 January 1959. Dickie was of course thrilled as he had always wanted to work in America. In 'Dors by Diana' she mentions that around this time occasional little upsets were creeping into the relationship. One of these she mentions was when comedian Jon Pertwee visited them one weekend and he and Diana went to visit an old cottage he was thinking of buying. Dickie became very jealous and refused to speak to them for hours.

Diana felt that the South African trip went well, and enjoyed the good weather and hospitality which she encountered everywhere. She was unaware that in England Dennis had been discharged from the London Clinic with the proviso that he took things easily, a warning he ignored, and within weeks he was re-admitted in a far worse condition. Diana rang him before her departure for the states and the Steve Allen Show and he did not sound good. When she told him that she would see him when she got back in about a month, he gave her the impression that he would not be alive by then.

The Steve Allen Show was a success and she was invited back for more guest appearances, all at a fee of $7,000 for each appearance. At the end of January 1959 Diana and Dickie decided to fly out to California for a holiday. For a few days she ignored the calls that were coming through from the press and even her agent. Finally film columnist Lionel Crane tracked her down on 31 January by placing a call to the Hollywood home of Roger Moore and his wife Dorothy Squires. Telling Dorothy not to divulge her whereabouts Diana went to the bedroom and picked up the extension to listen in to the conversation. She was to hear the devastating news that Dennis was dead. She immediately made arrangements to fly home which in 1959 took twenty four hours via Denmark.

On her arrival back home she had to face hordes of waiting pressmen. Damon Wise in 'Come by Sunday' said "Her tributes were hesitant and her criticisms strangely admiring. The good times still didn't outweigh the bad, but she couldn't find it in her heart to do the man down. They had been lucky charms for each other, she thought, each helping the other forward." Diana also had the surprise of learning that he had converted to Catholicism just a few weeks prior to his death. The funeral took place at 11am on 4 February 1959 at St James' Roman Catholic Church in Spanish Place, London W1. It was to be more like a star-studded premiere, as hundreds of people lined the streets outside the church, and inside it was packed to capacity as she silently walked to the front pew. With the priest talking in Latin it sounded to Diana like a scene for a continental film. In 'Dors by Diana' she said

"When the service ended and I was walking down the aisle, strange women grabbed me, shouting 'All right, Diana, we still love you' and other nonsensical things. One even asked me for an autograph! Outside, too, there was mild hysteria, with men and women crying and Dennis' parents sobbing, calling out my name as if somehow I might be able to bring him back…

I couldn't bear the thought of going to the cemetery; and anyway no-one had told me where it was! I felt like a stranger who had gate-crashed a party, only no-one was laughing the way they usually did at Dennis' parties. Not one of his male friends offered to help me, or find a taxi in which I could get away from the whole bizarre affair."

The day after the funeral she was to receive another shock when Jon Pertwee asked her to go to London and see him privately. He explained to her that a doctor friend of his had been working at the London Clinic and had been made privy to the real cause of Dennis' death. It had not been a heart attack but tertiary syphilis. Damon Wise in 'Come by Sunday' notes that "This is a dramatic but highly curious story. Why would a team of professional doctors not inform a dead man's widow of the potentially fatal disease she might be carrying – or, more bizarrely, leave the task to a friend of a friend?"

In 'Dors by Diana' she herself describes the revelation in more detail "Now I understood his continual insistence that he was going to die, which we all believed to be merely an over-emotional reaction. Dennis had been told the truth by his doctors, but pride would not allow him to discuss the nature of his disease."

On Jon Pertwee's advice she sought legal advice to find out what the situation was regarding a will. Diana was soon to find out how foolish she had been in leaving Dennis to manage her affairs "The taxman, too, was to become another grasping man in my life, and now that Dennis was dead his attentions were growing increasingly intense, thanks to the publicity about our vast fortunes in and out of England!"

Two weeks after the funeral found Diana, along with Dickie in New York, fulfilling her contract with Steve Allen. She returned to Britain at the end of February 1959 and the full details of Dennis' will had been published. All he had left – to his parents – was £800. All he had left Diana was debts of thousands of pounds to the Inland Revenue from the days when she believed he was attending to everything. The various properties and businesses such as the coffee bar 'El Toucan' were all in the hands of his various dubious business associates. Diana was the only person left to attack and therefore the obvious target for the taxman and the bankruptcy court. Quite rightly Diana felt that this was all very unfair as she had worked hard to achieve what she believed to be financial success. The cruel reality was now otherwise. Her only option was to secure what she had left. To this end she opened a trust, and allowed everything she owned to be placed in it, with Dickie, herself and any children they might have as the beneficiaries

18

Life With Dickie

Dickie's one thought now was marriage, and as soon as possible. Diana very much wanted the wedding to be in England with friends and family attending, but Dickie insisted that America was the place to have the ceremony and the arrangements were made for 9.30pm on 12 April 1959 at the New York apartment of Diana's American agent, Harry Steinman, before a Jewish Judge. This was followed by a large reception at a fashionable night club. In just eight weeks she had been an estranged wife, widowed and married again.

On their return to England Dickie busied himself with script writing for "The Diana Dors Show". It was of course a vehicle for Diana, but Dickie also took part and two American guests were flown over. Actress and singer Shirley Jones, who had starred in a number of films including the screen version of Rogers and Hammerstein's 'Oklahoma' and her husband Jack Cassidy, the father of 1970s pop idol David Cassidy. The show was a great success, and both Diana and Dickie were immediately signed to do a further show, which had to be postponed as Diana was to discover she was pregnant. She cancelled all forthcoming work dates and the Dawson's invested in a new home situated in Virginia Water in Surrey which Diana called 'Springwoods'.

Shortly before Diana became pregnant she had been approached by music publisher David Platz. Putting her in a studio with

Diana rehearsing with Dickie Dawson

bandleader Wally Stott, an album was recorded. When completed it would be sold to the highest bidder. This turned out to be Pye Records, and the album was released in February 1960 under the title 'Swingin' Dors'. It boasted a lavish cover with a swinging door gatefold front which opened outwards in two halves. The musical arrangements were very strong and Diana's voice carried the recordings beautifully.

Her first baby was due in February, so Diana went ahead and accepted bookings for an American tour which would start in March and run through to mid April. The press christened the baby 'The Cabaret Orphan'. Mark Richard Dawson was born at the London Clinic on 4 February 1960. Proud father Dickie presented Diana with a bracelet with the words 'Thank you for Mark Richard' inscribed on it.

She soon became aware of the fact that she was very much a working mother who within a month of Mark's arrival, had a contract negotiated for her by Dickie and her agent, for her to appear in Las Vegas at $7,000 a week, and also in England in a television drama, playing the role of a singer accused of murdering her lover. This was an episode in the Armchair Theatre series called 'The Innocent'. The part required her to sing two songs which she selected from the recently released album.

A company were planning to film Alan Sillitoe's novel 'Saturday Night and Sunday Morning' with a young up and coming actor called Albert Finney, and wanted Diana to play the leading female role opposite him. They had very little money however and could only offer £500. The low fee coupled with the fact that the leading man was unknown, and the added disinclination on Diana's part to act in an abortion scene, led her agent to turn down the part. It was something she always regretted as the film would herald the beginning of a new era in British films, and would have regenerated her professional reputation.

Money was to be the driving force in her career from now on, and Diana found herself appearing at the Dunes Hotel in Las Vegas, where the temperature was 119 degrees, on a well paid but punishing ten day booking. With her variety work up until now she had been used to doing two shows a day, in Vegas three was the norm. The first at 8pm, the second at midnight, and the third at 2am. She was a big success, and even before Variety magazine had written a glowing critique, the hotel had extended the contract until 4 August with a substantial rise in salary. Dickie revelled in the Vegas way of life, but Diana missed both her son and England terribly. Mark remained in Surrey with his nanny, so Dickie arranged for her to bring him over to the United States much to Diana's delight.

She had been with Dawson for just over a year and already he had changed. Gone was the charming witty man who could always make her laugh and in his place was a morose individual who would spend hours in his room, even when they had guests. Diana's cabaret profile was in the ascent and soon after the Dunes engagement Dawson took other cabaret bookings on her behalf. This included two weeks at the famous Ciro's club in Los Angeles.

In May 1960 her first autobiography 'Swingin' Dors' was published. The cover showed Diana in a strapless evening gown looking over her shoulder, in quotation marks it said "I've been a naughty girl!" Needless to say it flew off the shelves. Director Ken Hughes who had worked with her on 'The Long Haul' had plans to film her memoirs but it was decided that libel and censor problems would make things too difficult, so the project was abandoned.

Diana now made plans to move to the US full time. The decision was made not so much by herself but because of the threat of bankruptcy in England and the fact that she could earn more money in the States. An offer of £21,000 was made for the house and Dickie flew back to negotiate the terms and sell off most of the contents.

Film work was still being offered, but the days of the starring roles were over, and she accepted smaller parts in 'King of the Roaring Twenties' and 'On the Double' starring Danny Kaye. For this film she had her hair cut fashionably short for the first time in her career.

While Dickie negotiated the sale of the house in England, Diana purchased a property on Angelo Drive in Beverly Hills. The cost was $175,000 and it was considerably more than she could afford, but with the help of a mortgage and the capital from the sale of the property in England, it seemed the most sensible option. None of this, however, made any difference to their relationship and Dawson was becoming more and more of a stranger to Diana. When you feel lonely and vulnerable it is very easy to fall in love, and this is exactly what happened to her, while she was working on a television series called 'The Racers' starring a young actor called John Ashley. A passionate affair developed.

As Dickie had flown over to England to see his accountant, there were no obstacles in their way. However they had not reckoned with Mark's nanny Amy, who on Dickie's return informed him exactly what had been going on in his absence. This of course resulted in a very nasty scene. Ashley begged her to seek a divorce but she had very little time to think things through as she was off on a cabaret tour of South America. Diana went on the tour alone, but when she returned it was Dickie who met her at the airport carrying Mark, holding out a red rose to greet her. This made her feel guiltier than ever about the affair. Ashley withdrew from the picture and Dawson promised to show her more attention.

A London agent telephoned Diana with the offer of cabaret work there, and the thought of returning to England was so welcoming that she readily agreed. There was also a more practical reason for accepting the offer. In order to obtain their residents cards they had to leave America for short periods. They did not wish to become citizens, but all the time they were living there as aliens they were being heavily taxed. The contract Diana signed was with soho club king Paul Raymond. His famous Revue Bar which had opened in London's Brewer Street in 1958 began a new era of permissiveness. However, the venue Diana was contracted to appear at was far more up market. 'The Bel Tabarin' was a restaurant with floor show in London's Hanover Square.

Whilst performing at the Bel Tabarin she rented a mews house in West London. It was a contented time for her, made even more so by the fact that she was expecting her second child, who she wanted to be born in the United States. On 14 February 1962 she left London Airport for America, accompanied by Dickie, Mark, and his nanny. Her parting words were "I certainly won't be back this year". On 27 June 1962 at the Cedars of Lebanon Hospital in Hollywood she gave birth to her second son Gary who weighed in at 101b 2oz. Within ten weeks of Gary's birth, Dickie had her back in cabaret again, this time in Chicago, followed by two weeks in Las Vegas at the Riviera Hotel.

19

The Early Sixties

Diana flew back to Britain in January 1963 to play the role of Georgia in Michael Winner's film 'West 11'. The distinguished cast included Eric Portman, and the part Diana had revealed what talent she had as a serious actress. When filming wrapped, however, it was back to America and more cabaret.

She was performing at New York's International Club on 28 April when Dawson's agent called to say that her Aunt Kit had sent a cable to her home. The news was bad – Diana's father had died. The funeral had been arranged for the following Friday, but Aunt Kit did not put any pressure on her to attend. Instead Diana decided to continue her contract in New York. It was rather a heartless decision and one that she later regretted, although in her autobiography 'Dors by Diana' she says attending her father's funeral would have been out of a "sense of duty". This indicates that even when he died, Diana could not bring herself to love her father.

In spite of the birth of Gary, life with Dickie was becoming strained again. Diana's life was now a pattern of work and little else. She rarely saw the family she provided for and when she was home she would be there for only a few weeks. Her good friend Pamela Mason had said to her once that being a woman on her own and travelling the world she was bound to meet men who paid her compliments and treated her like a real woman. In New York that summer she became involved

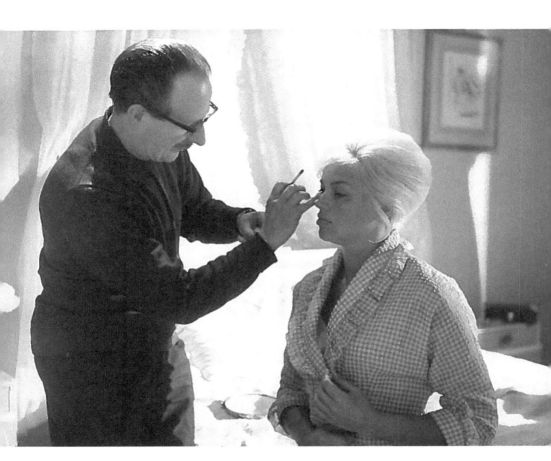

George Partleton checks Diana's make up on the set of "West 11"

Diana and Alfred Lynch between takes on the set of "West 11"

with a playboy named Frankie, a handsome Italian American. He had been married but was divorced. She began living life to the full with him, visiting all the smart clubs, restaurants and haunts frequented by the jet set. However there was one problem, in Diana's words "Frankie drank too much and it ruined many evenings". He wanted to marry her, but in her heart Diana knew she did not want to spend the rest of her life in jet set society. Leaving him a letter she made a hasty departure for the airport, as the news had come through that she had been booked for an upcoming tour of Australia which was a place she had never visited.

She naturally felt apprehensive, but her fears were unfounded and she settled in to rehearsing the Diana Dors show at Perth's leading theatre. On the bill with her was a singer named Darryl Stewart. Diana found herself impressed with both his talent and good looks. A friendship blossomed and then developed into an affair. At the end of the tour Diana was so besotted that she made plans for him to join her in America. She secured a flat just off Sunset Boulevard through Pamela Mason, and installed Darryl there for the next few months. Dickie learnt of the affair from a letter written by Stewart's wife. In the letter she included the information that she was about to give birth to their third child. Dawson went mad, confronted them both, and told Diana to get out of the house.

Pamela Mason told her she could stay with her and made an appointment for Diana to see her lawyer Marvin Mitchelson. One of the finest divorce lawyers in the business, he had brought Pamela one of the most lavish settlements in show business history. On his instruction Diana withdrew the money from their joint bank account and filed for divorce in January 1964. It was a decision she regretted almost immediately, and although Pam warned her that one day she would regret it, she withdrew the petition. She felt she could no longer trust Darryl, knowing that he had not only left his pregnant wife, but had concealed the fact from her.

As so often in her life during times of sadness, work came to the fore. She flew to England arriving on 8 March, principally to appear in a Sunday night TV play for ABC Television with William Franklyn called 'A Nice Little Business'. She also appeared in ABC's variety show

Diana as Grace Maxwell in "A Nice Little Business" (1964)

'Big Night Out', and slotted this in with a few weeks cabaret work in Selby, Manchester and Newcastle-upon-Tyne. The flights between Los Angeles and England were beginning to take their toll on Diana. She hated being in Hollywood and the gulf between her and Dickie was ever widening.

Her next film saw her returning to England for 'Allez France', an Anglo-French comedy. She played a film star which was not much of a challenge for her as an actress. The filming was at Shepperton Studios and, while there, Diana took stock. When it boiled down to it she was only working for the money, but what was the money paying for? A mortgage on a home she did not want, and for the future of her two children who she rarely saw because of the very fact that she was constantly working.

With thoughts in her mind about moving back to England at some future date, she rented a house in Chelsea on a six months lease. This she saw as a positive step for the future, but the more immediate plan was that it was a place she could be with Darryl Stewart, who had told her he was planning to leave his wife and join her in London. Plans for this were put in place, and then she received a letter from him in which he said he was unable to make it, but that one day he would. Diana wrote back giving him an ultimatum, she would not hear from him again for fifteen years.

The same night that she wrote to Darryl, Diana decided to throw a party to raise her spirits. Her old friend Dandy Kim was one of the guests, but it was a twenty six year old stranger who caught her eye. Troy Dante was a musician with a little known group which called themselves 'Troy Dante and the Infernos'. He infected Diana's weak spot with his ability to make her laugh. Within weeks he was a permanent resident in Diana's London home. In actual fact he was married, but she accepted this, and as far as the press was concerned she was his manager, getting bookings for the Infernos at cabaret venues where she herself was appearing. Diana loved the glamour of the pop world, seeing in it the magic Hollywood had once held for her as a child. Being with Dante meant she crossed paths with others from the musical scene including Leapy Lee, Jess Conrad, and later P J Proby, all of whom would become close friends.

Most of Diana's work now involved performing in working men's clubs. No film work was forthcoming, and the combination of the upkeep of house and family in Beverly Hills, and her own expenses, which now included Troy, meant she had little money to spare. She began to loathe the venues she had to play. No longer the sophisticated audience she had known in Las Vegas and other places, but audiences of men heckling and drinking beer and shouting lewd comments. As she commented in her 1981 autobiography "I was now prostituting my talent peddling a screen name that had once been big enduring shouts of "Get em off" or "Show us your tits".

October 1964 saw the release of a recording 'So Little Time' which she promoted on 'Thank Your Lucky Stars' hosted by Pete Murray. Towards the end of 1964 Diana signed a contract for pantomime. She was to play principal boy in a production of 'The Sleeping Beauty' being staged in Bromley. She was also able to persuade the management to find a small part for Troy in it, playing a strolling minstrel. Before rehearsals began she made a return to the States for a quick pre Christmas reunion, which she repeated in the New Year.

On her return to England there followed a project which could have completely turned her career round. In late 1964 Rediffusion television had approached her with an idea for a long running series to be called 'The Unusual Miss Mulberry'. She had signed a contract in the December to appear in it, reputedly for £30,000. Diana's character Kay Mulberry was the daughter of a high ranking officer at Scotland Yard who opens her own detective agency. At this time one of the most popular television programmes was the now legendary 'Avengers' with Patrick Macnee and Honor Blackman. It was thought that 'Miss Mulberry' would rival this.

Diana went on to film six hour long shows but the production was closed down after eight weeks. Little information was divulged as to the reason for this, other than 'legal complications'. The episodes that had been filmed were never broadcast, so no one really fully knew why the project floundered, whether it was really the legal complications, or just that executives at Rediffusion thought the programme not good enough to be broadcast.

All in all 1965 was a bad year for Diana, most of it revolving round working in nightclubs. She made a fleeting return to films with a small part in Michael Bentine's 'The Sandwich Man', a mainly silent comedy featuring a large cast of variety and character actors. Diana played a fishwife. As Christmas drew near she found herself back in pantomime once more as principal boy in 'Jack and the Beanstalk' this time in Bournemouth. In America Dickie had scored a hit in a new television series 'Hogan's Heroes', and as Diana was renting a house in Bournemouth for the festive season, he allowed the boys to visit.

20

Bankruptcy Looms As Alan Enters

The demands for income tax payments going back to her life with Dennis had become more than just a threat when she was presented with a bill for £48,000 just a few months later. At the time she had just moved in to a rented house with Troy. Called 'The Pavilion', it was situated in Sunninghill, Berkshire. The rent was 24 guineas a week. She had taken the lease on the property without really knowing where the money for the rent was coming from, as little work was on the horizon.

Her one film in 1966 was 'Berserk' starring the legendary Joan Crawford. Filmed at Shepperton Studios under the working title of 'Circus of Horrors', the story had Joan as the owner of a circus where a series of grisly murders were taking place. Diana's character Matilda was married to Lazlo (Philip Madoc) who had a sawing the lady in half act. Needless to say Diana came to an untimely end!

At thirty five years old Diana decided that she wanted a house of her own in England. She had come to the realization that working in California and living there with her sons was just not an option. The only problem was her financial situation. Her lawyer did not provide the advice she had hoped for, pointing out that with the threat of bankruptcy facing her, she should not own anything as it would be repossessed to cover her debts.

Diana went on to add a tax consultant to her list of advisors. As far as he was concerned the solution was simple. Sell the Beverly Hills

As Matilda in "Berserk" (1967)

home to clear the debt and then anything left over should be shared equally. This however is not what happened. Dickie came up with the alternative solution. As they had been separated for some time, the easy answer as far as he was concerned was a divorce, as long as she agreed to let him have the house, its contents, and legal custody of the children. By doing this it meant that the Inland Revenue would have no claim on the property as it would not be in Diana's name. In return for this, Dickie would allow her access to the insurance policies.

The decision was not an easy one for Diana but she realised there was little choice. However she made two stipulations. Firstly that she should have access to the boys at any time, and secondly that the American home should be put in trust for the boys, so that if Dickie should ever marry again they were ensured it was theirs. At the same time it was agreed that the money she had placed in a trust fund for Mark and Gary could be used to purchase a house. The house she decided on was to become her last permanent residence. Orchard Manor was a mock Tudor residence in Sunningdale and standing in three acres of land.

At the same time as the purchase of the house took place, Diana was offered a part in a film 'Hammerhead' with Vince Edwards in the lead. The fee from this enabled her to furnish the new home with the fittings it required. The debts were offset largely by club and personal appearances for which Diana was paid cash in hand, but then an interesting film script was offered to her. 'Baby Love' was based on the first novel of a young authoress called Tina Chad Christian. Diana was to play a tarty woman who commits suicide leaving her disturbed and sexually obsessed daughter (played by teenage starlet Linda Hayden) alone in the world. She hoped that this would lead to the big comeback part which would put her back at the top. Sadly this was not to be. When the film was released, apart from a suicide scene at the beginning, she was only seen in flashbacks and with no lines of dialogue.

On 31 May 1968 a bankruptcy receiving order was taken out against Diana. Several days a week she had to journey to London and sit for long periods in the tax consultant's office going over her whole life in readiness for the court case. A further meeting of creditors was held in the official receivers office on 5 July. Her fate was to be decided at

On location for "Baby Love" (1968) with Linda Hayden

a public enquiry on 3 October where she was to receive a forty-five minute investigation by senior official receiver Wilfred Whitehead. The questioning was detailed and went back to 1947 when she was a Rank contract artiste. The hearing was adjourned and Diana was ordered to return on 5 December when she would face further questioning.

In an interview with Clive Hirschhorn of the Sunday Express given in September 1968 she said "It's not the bankruptcy, and the litigations, and the bad publicity, and the scandals and all the things my name has been linked with that fill me with genuine despair but the mess I've made of my emotional life … and the failure of my marriage. These are the things that really hurt".

"And what makes me despair even further is the knowledge that it's highly unlikely I'll *ever* have a truly successful love affair. The fact that I'm in show business, which loads the dice against you anyway, and the fact that I've led a pretty hectic life, and that I'm a victim of my own image – oh, and all sorts of other neurotic things – makes it almost impossible to think about ever having a successful, happy love life. It's just one of those hard, cold facts you have to face sooner or later. And it makes the future look pretty bleak."

The future however was just about to take a turn for the better with regard to romance.

Alan Lake was a twenty-seven year old actor who originated from Stoke on Trent. His dark gypsy good looks made him natural casting as a villain. London Weekend Television had invested £150,000 in a new thriller series called 'The Inquisitors'. Lake and fellow actor Tony Selby were cast as two detectives who used psychology to solve crimes. It was to be the biggest break in his nine year career.

Diana's agent rang her to say that the producer Jim Goddard wanted her to make a guest appearance in the first episode. He visited her at Orchard Manor and explained that the part he wished her to play was that of a night club stripper called Sweet P. In the story she witnesses a crime but refuses to give evidence. The work was welcome from a financial point of view, but there was also the attraction of the leading man. When the producer mentioned the name Alan Lake, her mind went back to an ITV half hour theatre programme called 'Thief' in which he had played the lead, and she had been impressed with what she had seen. However the feeling was not reciprocated by Lake. When told who the guest star in the pilot episode was to be, his immediate reply was "Oh no not madam tits and lips" Alan belonged to the new wave of actors such as Richard Harris and Peter O'Toole and as far as he was concerned Diana belonged in the past.

The first day's rehearsal was on October 10 1968 in a Territorial Army Hall just off of Bond Street. Lake expected her to arrive in mink surrounded by her entourage and throwing a tantrum. He was in for a big surprise. When he arrived Diana was already there sitting on a chair reading her script. No entourage and no mink. Instead she was simply dressed in a low key woolen two-piece and a red leather coat with her blonde hair gently cascading over her shoulders, looking, as always, totally gorgeous.

When Jim Goddard brought him over to meet Diana he said "This is Alan. He calls you madam tits and lips". Alan was mortified but Diana just laughed. He was surprised to find how down to earth and funny she was. She in turn was equally impressed with his wit and zest for life. She said later that meeting him was like being hit by an express train. When they broke for lunch they went to a nearby pub together. Alan had read nothing about her in the papers so was surprised when she revealed that she was divorced. The next day after rehearsals they went out to dinner together and then on to the 'Colony' a famous club in the heart of London where they stayed until after closing time. Alan would later recall that "the staff were piling up the furniture around us. We hardly noticed. We only had eyes for each other". His opinion of film stars in general and Diana in particular had now changed. Her first readings in the rehearsal room had impressed him greatly as had her witty conversational skills.

The next day Alan proposed to her and made this official a few weeks later on 29 October 1968 when he presented her with a Mexican antique silver and amethyst ring. His uncle presented it to him shortly before he died on the understanding that Alan would promise to give it to the girl he was going to marry. Looking back in 1981 Diana said "Things truly had taken a crazy turn. Here I was in love with a man I had only just met, wearing his ring and knowing he loved and wanted me as much as I did him".

Shortly after the engagement the BBC broadcast a one hour play on 8 November 1968 called 'Where have all the Ghosts Gone?' If anyone still thought of Diana as a sex kitten the illusion was now shattered as in this she played a bitter, middle aged alcoholic woman who blames her teenage daughter for her husband's death and tries to ruin the girl's forthcoming marriage.

Diana married Alan on 23 November 1968 at Caxton Hall in the same room in which she had married Dennis Hamilton seventeen years before. The bride wore white lace and the groom black velvet. The reception took place at London's Astor Club and continued the whole weekend.

The following month saw Diana back in court for the bankruptcy hearing on 6 December. Sixty five minutes of gruelling questions left Diana feeling both humiliated and angry with herself for being so naïve and finally admitting "I never read letters properly. I have been downright irresponsible right down through the years, and that's why I'm in the mess I am today." She did not know who was gloating about her situation more, the taxman or the media, who were out in force as she left court.

She returned home to Alan at Sunningdale who had been a tremendous support to her throughout this stressful time. Unlike Dennis, he was not interested in her money, being a talented actor himself. Diana had told a journalist shortly before their marriage that she was convinced he would be earning more money than her in the not too distant future.

Sadly her words were not to come to fruition as in January 1969 London Weekend Television announced that "The Inquisitors" was to be scrapped before a single episode had been screened. They were pleased with the cast and everyone was paid, but it had just not lived up to expectations.

Within two months of the wedding, Diana became pregnant and it was announced in January that she would be having a baby in the autumn of 1969. Their son Jason was born on 11 September at a London nursing home and weighing 71b 14oz.

Diana with husband Alan Lake

Act Three

21

The West End At Her Feet

In early 1970 Alan received the script of a new work by playwright Donald Howarth called 'Three Months Gone', which was to preview at the prestigious Royal Court Theatre in London's Sloane Square. Diana was also sent a copy, but she found the piece confusing and asked the playwright to explain it to her, but he didn't or wouldn't. She recalled "Happy at home, enjoying playing the role of wife and mother for the first time in my life, I would have been perfectly content to stay that way. But the producer and author asked our mutual agent if I would read the script too. Frankly, neither of us liked it at all, feeling it to be a very involved, artistic piece, confusing and not particularly commercial. But they were amazingly persistent, even to the extent of coming to the house to implore us to accept the roles offered."

Diana's character, Mrs. Hacker was a loud mouthed sexually greedy widow approaching the menopause, with Alan playing one of her lodgers. 'Three Months Gone' opened on 28 January 1970 and was a great success, with her performance receiving great reviews. The Observer theatre critic said "All these plaudits for Miss Dors show an image can dog you all your life. She's been lumbered as a sex-pot since she made her first film, when she was fifteen. She tried to shake out from time to time. Her portrayal of a condemned woman in *Yield to the Night* in 1956 thrilled the critics but not the producers. As she says, she was the nearest thing to sex the British cinema had then and it didn't

151

want to part with a good thing. Kenneth Tynan directed her first stage play back in 1953. And it looks like the career of Miss Dors has changed in this direction once more."

Alan also received glowing reviews, and Sir Laurence Olivier was just one of their fellow thespians who rushed round backstage to congratulate them. As Diana said "When you have done a life time's cheesecake, the status you get from a "well done" kiss from Olivier is really something."

The play's success resulted in a transfer to the Duchess Theatre in the West End and a flood of offers for Diana who was soon to fly out to Germany for a film directed by Polish Director Jerzy Skolimowski called 'Deep End', and set in a London Public Baths with Jane Asher and John Moulder-Brown playing attendants at the bath house. Diana's character was a predatory female customer who attempts to seduce John Moulder-Brown in her private cubicle at the baths. She gave a very strong performance proving further still what a versatile actress she was. Looking back at her scene in 2011 Jerzy Skolimowski recalled:

"Talking about Diana Dors, I must say that her participation in the film was entirely my idea. Of course I fancy her as a young man, seeing her in her earlier films she was literally sex bomb! She was so beautiful, so sexy, and so attractive that she made an impression on me. The scene is actually quite serious because it is practically a rape scene done in a very camouflaged manner. The censorship at that time could have really put the scissors into that scene but because it was camouflaged by talking about football we managed to get it through. She improvised perhaps one third of the lines or maybe even half of her performance was improvised and how fantastically. Thanks to her sense of humour and really greatness, she let me use her in a way not many actresses would go for, you know in a really grotesque way. I am happy that the scene was not censored."

The bubble of success and happiness was about to burst however. Sundays were always at home days for Diana and Alan. She loved nothing better than preparing a traditional roast for dinner and Alan would usually pop down to the local hostelry for a pre lunch time drink. On Sunday July 12 1970 they had visitors for the day. Pop star 'Leapy Lee' Graham and his wife Mary who lived nearby. Leapy and Alan had become good

friends and often met up for a game of darts and a drink at the local. Unfortunately on this particular Sunday they became involved in a brawl at the Red Lion. When they got home to Orchard Manor, having been treated at hospital for minor injuries, they were too inebriated to give a satisfactory explanation as to what had occurred. Later in the day the Police arrived and they were both taken to Windsor Police Station for questioning. The outcome was that there would be a court case.

Diana had just persuaded Dickie to let Mark and Gary visit England, and she was concerned that the publicity generated by the incident might make him change his mind. Everything went to plan however, and although Alan had to appear at the magistrate's court, they remained unaware of the situation. In the pipeline for Diana now was a comedy series for Yorkshire Television called 'Queenie's Castle.' This had been specially written for her by Keith Waterhouse and Willis Hall. Alan was to have a main role in it too playing her brother in law.

The case was due to be held at Reading Assize Court on October 16th. Although nervous, both Alan and Diana were quietly confident about the outcome. He had no criminal record and he was pleading guilty which his lawyer said would help his case. The court heard how Lee and Lake had been playing darts with other customers. Alan bought a round of drinks for 15s 0d. Anthony Slack, the relief manager said he would take another 3 shillings for the Moussec which Lake had the day before.

The prosecuting council said that a row followed with Lake claiming that the Moussec had been on the house. Leapy Lee threw a glass of beer over the manager and a fight began. Witnesses said that Lake produced a flick knife and gave it to Lee, who rushed at the manager lunging at his stomach. Mr Slack moved sideways and was stabbed in the arm, necessitating eighteen stitches in hospital. Having heard all the evidence Mr Justice Everleigh was not impressed and both received Prison sentences. Lee Graham received three years and Alan Lake eighteen months. They also both received nine month sentences to run concurrently for damage to the property. The bottom had fallen out of Diana's world. She had a car waiting to take them both up to Leeds to begin work on 'Queenie's Castle' but instead Alan was taken down to the cells and Diana had to continue to the north alone.

As so often during her life, Diana found consolation in her

professional work. She adored the role of Queenie Shepherd. Queenie was a straight talking blowsy woman who lived in a tower block with her three idle sons and brother in law. Her husband was AWOL supposedly working on the roads. The role of her brother in law, originally intended for Alan, was taken over by Tony Caunter. Diana said at the time "Everyone's been a brick and so nice especially Tony."

Diana as Queenie Shepherd surrounded by the local children
"Queenie's Castle" (1972)

December 1970 saw Alan moved to Verne Prison on Portland Bill in Dorset, and in the new year of 1971 on January 21 an appeal was heard. In spite of glowing testimonials from Lord Olivier and others, it was turned down. Diana had no choice but to soldier on with her professional work. In February 1971 she went off to Spain to film a western 'Hannie Caulder' starring Raquel Welch as a woman taking revenge on the men who killed her husband.

Cabaret work was fortunately in abundance and she found herself working all over England in the following months. In between she made a six hour journey each month to visit Alan in prison. In her handbag she carried a calendar ticking off the days till his release. Due to his good behaviour in prison Alan was released to her earlier than expected. He earned himself a six month remission and was released on October 16 1971.

Diana arranged a welcome home party for him with a host of friends back at Orchard Manor, and had a very special gift for him. As a token of her love she presented him with a beautiful horse. A seventeen-hand mare called Sapphire. Alan was signed to work with Diana almost immediately after his release on a production of 'Dixon of Dock Green' for the BBC. His part was that of a lodger in a boarding house with Diana playing his landlady. Sadly this success was not to last, when Alan's career took another blow in February 1972.

When he was out riding Sapphire in Windsor Great Park he crouched down to avoid the overhanging branch of a tree. Unfortunately the horse reared up at precisely the wrong moment and Alan took the full force of the branch thrust at him, resulting in two broken vertebrae, his shoulder and a rib. Luckily the helmet he was wearing prevented a fractured skull. He was kept in hospital for three weeks before doctors allowed him to go home. He still suffered pain when walking and had to return to the hospital for traction, but he was lucky to be alive.

Diana making a personal appearance in South London in 1972

Diana making a personal appearance in South London in 1972

22

Professional Highs And Personal Lows

Actor and Director Lionel Jeffries who Diana had worked with before in the fifties on the play 'Man of the World', was preparing a new film. He had had a very successful directorial debut with 'The Railway Children' in 1970, and was going to follow this up with another project aimed at the family market called 'The Amazing Mr. Blunden'. The part Diana was offered 'Mrs Wickens' was a wicked, conniving wart ridden harridan whose evil plot to kill two children is foiled by two other children who travel back in time to help them. Diana adored playing the character as it really tested her ability as an actress and had nothing to do with her sexy image past and present. Lionel Jeffries, talking about her role in the film in 1990, said "At the press show, I promise you this is true, she came on with the mop cap and the wart and it said 'Mrs Wickens, Diana Dors', and I guarantee there were sixty hard bitten journalists who went 'I don't bloody believe it, Di Dors, that was Dors?!'"

Lionel and his wife were Roman Catholics, and were both surprised to learn that Diana and Alan were receiving instruction to enter the Catholic faith. They warmly agreed to sponsor the Lake's transition. After a year of instruction and debating they were accepted into the church at a small private ceremony at the Church of the Sacred Heart in Sunningdale in the spring of 1974. The reason for the conversion was never made clear by Diana. Damon Wise writing

"The Amazing Mr Blunden" as the evil Mrs Wickens

in 1998 said "For her part, Diana was perhaps looking for something to hold on to through the rough times."

There were certainly more of these ahead. Almost a year after Alan's horse riding accident, Diana was admitted to hospital after falling down some steps outside a nightclub in Wakefield where she had been appearing in cabaret. Alan rushed to the hospital where she had been taken to make arrangements for her transfer nearer to home for an operation, as she needed to have a pin placed in her leg. She was laid up for three months and towards the end of the period she received an offer to go to Sweden for a film. The producers said that if she was still not walking properly they were happy for her to play the character from a wheelchair.

More sadness followed as her Aunt Kit passed away. She had been living in their former home in Marlborough Road and the property now passed to Diana. It held memories for her, but memories were of little use, so she decided to sell it. There was no point in living in the past.

Following on from 'Queenie's Castle' came another television vehicle for Diana called 'All Our Saturdays'. This time she played a Yorkshire woman called Di Dorkins who manages an amateur rugby team. It was sadly not a great success, but Diana enjoyed working in the television medium and her ambition was to have her own talk show. In the summer of 1973 her wish was granted with the pilot of a new pet chat show with the rhyming title 'Paws for Dors.' The guest stars were Dudley Moore, Zsa Zsa Gabor and the Marquis of Bath. A series did not follow, but in December she received some very exciting news which was to raise her profile considerably. Keith Michell announced that she would be playing Jocasta opposite his Oedipus in 'Oedipus Tyrannus' at the prestigious Chichester Festival Theatre. The role of Queen Jocasta, a mythical matriarchal ruler, who marries her son Oedipus, after he has murdered his father, was a real challenge for her acting abilities.

The casting stunned the newspaper critics, and Diana knew she was going to have to work harder than she ever had before to impress them. When the play was staged in June 1974 reviews were mixed. One described her as "splendid" another that "she brings genuine humanity to the production" whilst Express critic Herbert Kretzmer said "The best that can be said for her is that she's a game girl." As always, Diana took reviews in her stride.

"Oedipus Tyrannus" as Jocasta with Keith Michell as Oedipus.
Chichester Festival Theatre (1974)

When Oedipus ended Diana went on to play another character part on television in ATV's 'Thriller' series, 'Nurse Will Make it Better'. Diana played an evil 'nurse' who through Black Magic makes well again the daughter of an American diplomat who has been paralysed following a riding accident. In the final scenes she reveals herself as the devil. Filming began in October 1974. Diana had always believed in black magic and the forces of evil, and several unexplained incidents during the filming made her wish she had not taken part. On the drive up to Elstree studios for the filming she witnessed a fatal car crash, following a freak rainstorm the set was flooded, and a prop crucifix mysteriously snapped in two.

Worse was to come though. After filming wrapped she was looking forward to settling down to a normal home life again with Alan and Jason who was now five years old. She was also looking forward to celebrating her sixth wedding anniversary. On November 23 she felt unwell and after tea she told Jason's nanny that she had a headache, and her body ached as well. She had an aspirin and took herself off to bed early. The next morning Diana felt just as unwell, and believing it to be flu decided to stay in bed. Around midday Alan heard her call out. Rushing upstairs he found her threshing around in bed and holding her head in agony. The doctor was called for and by 2pm she was on her way to the London Hospital for Neurological Diseases, where meningococcal meningitis was diagnosed. With Diana lying in a coma, the doctors told Alan that they held out little hope and that she would probably not last the night. However her amazing inner strength came through and she regained consciousness at around midnight.

Over the next few days in hospital she received enormous quantities of bouquets, cards and telephone calls including one from the legendary Joan Crawford who she had worked with on the film 'Berserk.' Many people who contract meningitis suffer debilities such as deafness, blindness or paralysis as a result. Miraculously Diana's recovery was total.

Within seven weeks Diana was back rehearsing for a play. Both she and Alan were offered a tour of 'Murder Mistaken' by Janet Green. This had been made into the film 'Cast a Dark Shadow' in 1955 starring

Margaret Lockwood and Dirk Bogarde. The male lead role was a wonderful opportunity for Alan, and she felt it would be good for them to act together again after their previous success in 'Three Months Gone'. Her hopes were not realised. As she said in 1981 "The tour was disastrous from beginning to end. Alan drank all night and every night after the show. So much for my thinking, as I had on reading it, that the demanding role would sap his boundless energy. On the contrary, his adrenalin became even more charged."

Following her discharge from hospital Diana was put on medication and found her body clock very unsettled. The mystery was solved early in the New Year when she discovered she was pregnant. The baby was due in October 1974 but due to her age and the health problems she had suffered her doctor felt that perhaps a termination would be a wise course of action. She agreed and he arranged for her to visit a private clinic in Brighton for the operation, but come the day she could not go through with it. "I was forty-four years old, a dangerous time! But how could I, as a Catholic, go to mass, receive Holy Communion and pretend to be a Christian if I committed murder?"

Diana was looking forward to being a mother again, and regarded the baby as "the great gift of my tranquil middle age." She felt both fulfilled and lucky at last. During the summer she began to feel unwell and towards the end of the summer her blood pressure became high. She could not feel any movement from the baby, and at a check up doctors could not feel a heartbeat, but they feared termination in case the baby was alive. Diana went into labour on 28 August and was taken to Westminster Hospital. Alan was beside her at the birth. What should have been one of the happiest moments in their life turned out to be the most tragic for the baby boy was still-born.

"Murder Mistaken" (1975) as Freda Jeffries with Alan Lake as Edward Bare

23

Accomplished Actress And Writer

No marriage is easy, and Diana and Alan were now entering one of the most difficult phases of theirs. All of the problems they had gone through, Alan's prison sentence, his accident, and Diana's meningitis had brought them closer together but had camouflaged one very serious problem, that of Alan's drinking. Diana's great inner strength had helped her through at the loss of their baby, but he was unable to cope and turned to alcohol for comfort.

As his drinking bouts became more regular, Diana decided to seek professional help. When Alan was diagnosed as an alcoholic, she did everything in her power to help him

She finally made him see that he had a problem and he agreed to go into hospital to an Alcohol Treatment Unit. When he returned they experienced three and a half months of perfect happiness, but then in the summer of 1976 the news that his Mother had cancer caused a relapse. Court appearances on drunk and disorderly charges, ejections from restaurants and clubs, and nights spent sleeping in ditches followed. At one point Diana left Orchard Manor taking Jason with her and went to stay with friends in Brighton. Whilst there however news reached her that Alan was seriously ill. She returned to Sunningdale to find him dehydrated and near to death. Carried out of Orchard Manor on a stretcher he was admitted to the same hospital for treatment.

In early 1974 Diana had flown over to America to visit sons Mark and Gary. Dickie had never got over the acrimony of the divorce and had remained bitter towards her with the result that she had no worthwhile relationship with her boys. There was never any acknowledgment of letters, birthday or Christmas presents she sent them. She soon discovered the reason for the lack of thank yous; her boys never received her communications or gifts. She suspected that the nanny, Amy was responsible for this. Due to her serious illness followed by the pregnancy and subsequent loss of her baby, the only chance Diana had to return was in January 1976.

Alan flew out with her along with Jason who Mark and Gary had not seen for six years. Both boys had grown considerably since she had last seen them. "There, waiting for us at Los Angeles airport, stood two grown-up boys, or so it appeared, for at sixteen and fourteen both looked very sophisticated." Amy had died the previous June and Diana hoped that relations with her sons would now improve. Dickie, now established as a television star, was a different person, positive and full of self respect. Diana returned to England happy and confident for the future.

1977 was not a golden year for the Lakes artistically. Alan did voice overs for various drinks companies advertising and played the part of Franz Schubert in advertisements for 'Kronenberg' beer "summer's rich madness is spent." After her serious classical venture as Jocasta in 'Oedipus Tyrannus', all that came Diana's way were bit parts in ribald sex comedies 'Keep it up Downstairs', 'Adventures of a Taxi Driver', and 'Adventures of a Private Eye.'

The 1970s saw a decline in the British Film Industry and the Rank Organisation were to cease production altogether in the summer of 1980. Many of the films fell into three distinct categories. Cheap horrors, big screen adaptations of television comedy series, or smutty sex romps. Prior to the 'Adventures' films, Diana had appeared in the other two categories in 'Theatre of Blood' with Vincent Price, and 'Steptoe and Son Ride Again' with Harry H Corbett.

She hated the way the British Film Industry was heading. Most of the scripts she was sent she turned down as they were mainly pornographic, some wanting her to remove her clothes. "I've never

Diana on the set of "Keep it up Downstairs"

done that and never will. I know I was a sex symbol, but we knew how to be daring without having to show too much."

To maintain her beautiful home, pay school fees and keep the Inland Revenue happy, Diana had to find something else to bring more money into the coffers. In 1974 she had written a piece for Woman's Own and had hankered after writing a book herself ever since. The time now seemed right, but she did not wish to write an autobiography at this stage of her life. Instead she decided to recall stories about herself and others she had worked with in the entertainment business.

She converted Jason's nursery into an office. To help her to recall specific incidents she covered the walls with photographs of herself with such legends as Jack Benny, Bob Hope, Doris Day, Ginger Rogers and Liberace, as well as stills from her films, covering the thirty years she had spent in the world of entertainment.

Performance-wise she was just about to embark on another great character part, namely Mrs Bott in a television series based on Richmal Crompton's 'Just William' books. Her daughter Violet Elizabeth was played by Bonnie Langford, and Jason appeared as one of the members of William's gang, the Outlaws. Diana loved the part saying "Mrs Bott is great fun to play. I can be as vulgar as I like. The Botts are real hypocrites, the sort of terrible people I have always detested."

January 1978 saw Diana on a promotional tour for the forthcoming book 'For Adults Only.' It was due for general release on February 14 – Valentines Day. This was a day she and Alan always spent together and on this particular one she handed him a poem she had written which was to become one of his most treasured possessions

What is a Lake?

"A Lake is a child-man who can never find the right clothes to wear at the right time, likes you to bathe and dry him, wash his hair and spoil him endlessly.

He is a wonderful mixture of different things at different times, a man of many moods, loaded with personality, talent and sex appeal, shy and quiet *sometimes*, wild, uninhibited and defiant *most* times.

A Lake can learn a whole play without study by merely using his photographic memory – yet can never remember people's names, or the places he is supposed to be at or how to get there.

A Lake will quote Dylan Thomas at random, read Shakespeare aloud half-way through the night, drink too much, shout too much, and more than likely have a punch-up with anyone who challenges him, but give him a comic book and a bottle of pop in bed, and you'll never hear another sound all evening.

He is super-sensitive, domineering, amusing, generous, egotistic, intelligent, sadistic, sweet and understanding. An exhibitionist with black curls which never go where they have been combed to go, dark sad eyes, and a smile which will charm the birds from the trees! One minute a reincarnated pirate complete with gold earring, flickering his sabre, another minute a little boy lost, desperate for love and affection.

A Lake will aggravate, irritate and annoy you, fascinate, captivate and dominate you, worry you, protect you and comfort you, but *never* bore you. He is jealous, overpowering and larger than life, but he has the insecurity of a ten-year old!

A Lake can never sleep! Will keep you awake all night, for he is afraid of the dark and in the morning when he has deliberately woken you from a rest you *may* have been lucky enough to get, he will go off to sleep himself, leaving you to sit staring into space wondering what to do next.

His mind is a fabulous structure of experiences and many pieces of knowledge, once learned and never forgotten. If he loves you then you are indeed favoured, but if he hates you, he will never let you forget why, and neither will he!

He is quick tempered, quick witted, and quick to know if he has hurt you, but it takes him half an hour to put his clothes on in the mornings, and he can only concentrate on *one* thing at a time, so if he is watching television and you ask a question, don't expect an answer.

Invite him to a cocktail party, and you will get a refusal, but he will spend all day and night at the local drinking beer and playing darts.

A Lake will sing, dance, play the drums, mouth organ and spoons, mimic brilliantly, and act anyone off the stage, he will also shoot, fence and play cards at any time. He is passionate, unselfish and a *very* consistent lover, and if you can keep up with him you are quite a person. I try, and often fail, but in spite of this for some strange and mysterious reason, known only to him, he loves me.

What is a Lake?

He is above everything the man I worship and love."

February and March 1978 saw Diana marketing her book and Alan being offered a part in a film. The production was called 'Playbirds' and the star was adult movie queen of the time Mary Millington. Alan's part was that of a sex magazine editor whose female models are being systematically murdered, with Millington playing the role of a police officer who goes undercover as a model to lure the killer out of hiding. Diana was naturally unhappy about the type of film it was, but she had been in show business for a number of years, and fully realised that it was work and if you needed it, no matter what it was, you had little choice but to accept it. Alan of course was happy to have a film after the lean times he had experienced in recent years, and hoped that it would lead to more work.

The film was released in the autumn of 1978 and was an immediate success at the box office with the result that both he and Mary Millington were signed up for a sequel 'Confessions from the David Galaxy Affair'. In this Alan played a fraudulent astrologer, whose crooked past life catches up with him. Millington provided the sex interest in the guise of Millie, a frigid young woman who is sent to Galaxy to be cured.

Diana was delighted that Alan had been offered more work, and she herself was offered a part in it. In the story Galaxy lived in a luxurious flat owned by a rich woman named Jenny Stride, and this was the part Diana undertook along with singing the vocal for the opening and closing credits. Diana had previously worked on another film in which Mary Millington featured 'Keep it up Downstairs' (1976) and she liked her. There were two traits in people that Diana could not abide, hypocrisy and dishonesty. Mary was totally upfront and honest about her profession and Diana admired her for this with the result that they became good friends. Mary tragically died from an overdose on

19 August 1979, her funeral taking place in Holmwood Surrey on 24 August. Both Alan and Diana attended. The tragedy made Diana reflect on how much the glamour business had changed since her hey day in the 1950s, but some things remained the same – another unhappy sex symbol was in the grave.

24

Autobiography At Fifty

Diana's main work in early 1979 was another book 'Behind Closed Dors', a sequel to 'For Adults Only', and following the same A-Z format. Her publisher set up another tour to promote the work and this one proved more extensive, even taking in Australia.

Alan's drinking was still a problem and reaching crisis point around this time. Gary flew over from America to stay with Diana in February 1979 and Alan took him and Jason to Blackpool to see the illuminations for Jason's tenth birthday. The visit was to prove a disaster. They were staying at the four star Imperial Hotel where TUC delegates were also in residence for a conference. Alan, after a heavy drinking session became verbally abusive to them with the result that he was thrown out of the bar. He then tried to gain entry to a nearby nightclub. When he was refused entry due to his inebriated condition, he produced a knife and waved it at the bouncers. The next day sober and full of remorse he was fined £150 for possession of an offensive weapon.

Diana was now a best selling authoress and recognised as an accomplished actress. She had one ambition that she had not yet achieved. During her career she had been a guest on many chat shows hosted by luminaries such as Michael Parkinson and Russell Harty. Now she desperately wanted to host one of her own. With her strong personality and show business background she felt that she had an advantage over most chat show hosts, many of whom came from a journalistic background. "Showbiz folk like me hold a mirror to life. My profession contains some of the most sympathetic people in the world. We are interested in others. We observe. We study. We understand. And another thing – I speak English beautifully which is more that you can say for Mike (Parkinson) and Russell (Harty)."

Upon hearing that Southern Television were doing a series of pilot programmes for chat shows, she put her name forward. For her show she interviewed Mary Whitehouse and comedienne Judy Carne. The outcome was that she was offered six more thirty minute programmes all to be shown in the Southern Television area and called 'Open Dors'. She liked to be quite controversial with her choice of guests. She had Lord Montagu debating the future of the monarchy with anti royalist MP Willie Hamilton, and Lord Longford discussing pornography with Paul Raymond.

The success of her two A-Z books resulted in her publishers asking her to think about writing her life story. Having now got the bug to write more, she did not need much persuading and the early part of 1979 saw Diana busy writing her autobiography.

Alan's mother, Millicent Lake, died of cancer on January 25 1980. It affected everyone in the family but Alan more deeply as he had always been very close to her. He sought solace in the only way he knew – alcohol. Diana by now had reached the end of her tether in regard to his drunken behaviour, and she left him, taking Jason with her, and went to stay with friends in Brighton. Alan begged her to return, and when she did she found him in a crumpled heap against the living room wall. Diana told him that if he was sincere about wanting to give up the booze he would have to check in to a rehabilitation clinic again. This he agreed to, returning once more to Northampton. On his previous visit, like so many drinkers, Alan could not accept that he was an alcoholic, now the situation had changed.

When Diana visited him in the clinic she told him that she could not have him at home again. Alan assured her that this time his recovery would be total and that he would never touch another drop. He asked her to give him two weeks, and then if he failed he would go away. Diana agreed. The first thing he did on returning home was to get in trim. After some lean years parts were beginning to come his way again, and he wanted to make the most of any opportunities. He went up to Northumberland to work on the television series 'Blake's Seven' and then in the successful 'Dick Turpin' starring Richard O'Sullivan in the title role. Diana herself landed a role in a two hour special of the series. It was a wonderful character part for her, playing a bawdy woman in charge of a gang of girls in a very suggestive wash house scene.

The British Film industry had begun to decline throughout the 1970s, and towards the end of the era very few films were being made. The Rank Organisation in particular had hit hard times, and closed down their film production operation in June 1980. Having been discovered by Rank, Diana found this news very distressing, and said at the time:

"It's like someone dying. The British film industry was something of a joke until this flour millionaire came along and created a great new industry. They controlled Denham, Pinewood and what are now the BBC television studios at Lime Grove.

Many big stars of the films have died or settled in America or on the continent, but there's still a wealth of talent here that could make wonderful films. But people these days seem only to want to watch porn films, sex and violence – and that's where the money is. It's terribly sad."

Following the success of her chat programme for Southern Television – 'Open Dors', she was offered a six part ITV lunchtime 'conversation' programme called 'The Diana Dors Show.' The shows focused on a different theme each week including style, fortune telling, and 'what turns a woman on.' The programmes were aimed at working housewives, and as well as interesting discussions it was Diana's intention to bring some glamour to the screen again, wearing dresses which were specially designed for her, with her neck, arms and fingers adorned with expensive jewellery.

Writing her autobiography was taking up a lot of her time, but she still kept busy in all aspects of performance. She made many guest star appearances on various comedy shows and panel games, in addition to various character parts in television dramas. The 'Hammer House of Horror' series saw her in an episode called 'Children of the Full Moon' undertaking the part of Mrs Ardoy, foster mother to a family of beautiful children who also happened to be werewolves.

"Children of the Full Moon" as Mrs Ardoy
with Christopher Cazenove as Tom

"Children of the Full Moon" with Celia Gregory
as Sarah and Christopher Cazenove

1981 even saw her on 'Top of the Pops' playing a glittering fairy godmother in the film to accompany pop sensation Adam Ant's hit song 'Prince Charming.' They had filmed at Shepperton Studios where she had made 'Lady Godiva Runs Again' back in the fifties and the memories came flooding back to her.

In October 1981, the month of her fiftieth birthday, 'Dors by Diana', her autobiography, was published. Her birthday was celebrated at a luxurious lunch in Kensington, hosted by her publishers, where she was very happy to answer questions about her age which she had never lied about anyway. When asked what it felt like to reach fifty she said simply "It's like waiting to go to the dentist. Once you get there, it's all right and you feel just the same." After the lunch she moved on to Skindles nightclub in Maidenhead accompanied by Alan, Jason and Gary. The birthday cake was shaped like a heart with iced giant breasts and mouth, reflecting back to the first meeting with Alan when she discovered he thought of her as 'madam tits and lips.'

Orchard Manor was always a lavish home. One of Diana's friends had referred to it as "Hollywood in Berkshire" and in 1981 work began on a swimming pool. Alan had come up with the idea as he knew how much Diana liked to swim, and it would be the finest money could buy. The pool had a public christening in December when show host Russell Harty visited Orchard Manor complete with camera crew to do a programme about it.

As the year drew to its close Diana felt that maybe she was coming back into fashion again. Margaret Thatcher had been Prime Minister for the past two years, and Britain was recovering from the seventies, where, governed by Labour, it had been crippled by both union disagreements and inflation, and heading for a short lived consumer boom.

In January 1982 she was interviewed by Clive Limpkin of the Sunday Times:

"My God, we've come through a lot" she said, and her eyes went big at the thought of it all. "There was Alan's prison sentence, and his alcoholism. Then he broke his back, and I nearly died from meningitis, and then I broke a leg, and our second child was still-born ... You know, I've done cabaret on US Air Force bases with them shouting things at me and beer cans rolling round my feet and I used to think to myself, this is just prostitution, living off a name. I'd been so used to being on top, and it was hard, it really hurt".

"But I'm not bitter, that's such a wasted emotion. I've had so many lives, so many back- cloths. When I breathe my last I won't feel bitter, all I'll think is now I'm finally going to get a darn good rest." And her head went back and she gave a laugh that would hush a pub.

She released a cover version of the Peggy Lee classic 'Where Did They Go?' on producer Simon Napier-Bell's Nomis label. On the flipside she recorded a duet with son Gary. The lyrics of 'Where Did They Go?' became especially poignant due to the tragedy in her life which was shortly to follow.

25

A Red Book And TVam

Diana was still working hard to pay the bills; in fact life was becoming work, work, and more work. On the morning of Thursday 24 June 1982 she was engaged to open a hotel, but awoke that day feeling unwell. She was suffering from acute stomach pains but being the consummate professional that she was, Diana soldiered on with the engagement, graciously shaking hands and smiling through gritted teeth. By the time she returned home the pains were worse, she collapsed on the stairs and was rushed by ambulance to the private Princess Margaret Hospital in Windsor.

Initially she was thought to have a burst appendix, but when they operated they discovered that an ovarian cyst had ruptured. The operation took three hours and the surgeon had to pass the bad news on to Alan. The cyst was malignant. Diana had cancer. A few days later the specialist told her the news as well. It took some time to sink in. "When they told me it was a terrifying jolt. No, no, no, I said, you've got it wrong. It can't happen to me … I'm not the cancer type."

Diana came through the surgery incredibly well but her Doctors advised her to relax and not take any work on board for at least six weeks. The operation and the revelation that she had cancer changed her perspective on life completely and she cleared her diary for the next few months, apart from filling in for Gloria Hunniford on her Radio 2 programme.

Following her surgery she had to check into Charing Cross Hospital for two days and nights every week for chemotherapy treatment. It was not a pleasant time for her as the treatment was severe and made her feel very ill, but she never complained and persevered with it, believing it was making her better.

At this time she was a columnist for the Daily Star newspaper, her column being called 'Sincerely Yours.' Following her surgery and treatment she felt it would help her better to understand the problems her readers faced. "I get all sorts of letters, some relating to illnesses. In the past I've had to refer the writers to a doctor. Now, I'll be able to give some first-hand knowledge."

In October 1982 Diana received an unexpected surprise, when she was chosen as a subject for television's 'This is Your Life' for the second time. When she entered the darkened auditorium of the Royalty Theatre in London's Kingsway, her first words to presenter Eamonn Andrews, as he led her down the stairs to the stage to tumultuous applause, were "Oh Eamonn, Oh you can't do this to me again"

As always Diana was very humble about her success, and when a still was shown of her as Mildred in her first film 'The Shop at Sly Corner' she retorted "oh how awful!', and when a clip from her second film 'Holiday Camp' was shown, Eamonn said "you went on to make many more films" her reply was "I don't know why!"

Alan was of course seated beside her and other members of both their families were present. Son Jason sat beside his father and there was a recorded message from Mark, Gary and Mark's wife Kathy. Some film had been made outside Paramount Studios but due to technical problems only the sound was able to be played. Mark said "Hi Mom, I hope you're having a great night, and I hope you're recording it all for when you come out to California again." Gary continued "its three months since I saw you and Alan and Jason. I really miss you and love you all. When I talked to you last it was great to hear you were back to your old self again. When you were taken ill you really gave us such a big scare. I've been thinking of all the things I kept meaning to put in all those letters I kept meaning to write." A small piece of film followed with Mark, Gary and Kathy waving goodbye. Diana wiped back the tears.

She was soon full of happiness again as members of the 1946

London Academy of Music and Dramatic Art class appeared on stage finishing with comedy actress Pat Coombes who said "Ere Di do you remember at LAMDA" to which she replied "I never forget! You were the comedienne and I was the bad girl." Memories of her Rank Charm School days came flooding back with those she had worked with arriving. John Blythe from the 'Huggetts' films and 'A Boy a Girl and a Bike'. followed by Megs Jenkins and Morris Denham who had both featured in the latter, along with Patrick Holt who had also played her husband in 'Miss Tulip stays the Night.' Finally there was Olive Dodds who had run the charm school, and who Diana had not seen for twenty two years.

There was also Dr Desmond Morris from her Swindon days who thanked her for the pin up pictures she had sent him when he was a young subaltern, and close friend and fellow actor Lionel Jeffries who had directed her in the film 'The Amazing Mr Blunden'. Talking about her performance in this he said "She received national and international acclaim for that performance as she proved once more as she's always doing, what a marvellous exclusive actress she is. She's not just a good actress, she's a totally exclusive and brilliant actress, and I love her very much."

Comedy legend Bob Hope re-iterated this thought saying "I love you a lot, and these days there's quite a lot more of you to love. In fact you're the only bit of the British Film industry that's expanded!" Fellow actor Alfred Marks, who had appeared with her in Oedipus at Chichester, said of the production "this was probably the biggest tragedy in Greek theatre and we had more laughs on that than any comedy I've ever done in my life." Diana replied with a beaming smile "thanks to you!"

World famous entertainer Liberace was also full of praise for her saying "I have such fond memories of you Diana when you first came to California, back in the days when we were both sex symbols" and went on to recall the wonderful memories of those times concluding with "I am so proud of the fact that you have become such an accomplished actress." The biggest surprise of the evening was saved until last with the actual appearance of Mark and Gary along with Mark's wife Kathy. Diana quite naturally broke down in tears.

May 1983 saw an announcement that Diana would be joining the network television station TVam. The launch of the channel had not been without problems, but thanks to the inventiveness of producer Greg Dyke and the introduction of puppet rodent "Roland Rat" viewing figures were on the increase. One of his ideas was to introduce a diet slot into the programme, and knowing Diana to be one of the most popular actresses and celebrities on television, he felt she would be the ideal person to appear in the feature.

In October 1983 Diana would celebrate her 52nd birthday and the idea was that she would shed 52 pounds in weight, one pound for each year of her life. Her lifelong friend Michael Caborn-Waterfield had come up with the x-cel slimming programme. The diet was based on 1,000 calories a day, incorporating recipes containing foods high in both fibre and gelatine. Diana also had the support of twelve other people who were joining her on the slim in. Miss Dors and her fellow dieters weighed in at the prestigious Cannons Sporting Club on Friday June 28. Her weight registered at 15 stone 3 pounds.

Anne Diamond one of TVam's presenters at the time reflected back in 2000 "It was the very beginning days of TVam and one of the ideas was to bring in Diana Dors to do a dieting spot, and you knew the minute you heard that that it would be a success, and it was a terrific success. She used to come in on the Friday and then there would be this saga where she was meant to actually talk live about the diet that she was on, give the audience tips on what sorts of foods to cook for themselves, how to do it on a budget, things like that. Things about which Diana knew nothing at all – and you could tell!"

"None of us were really convinced that Diana was ever really on a diet but she did used to lose about a pound a week, but it was because she took off jewellery. She wore huge jewellery, and she'd just take off a bracelet and a couple of rings, slip off her slippers, get on the scales, and hey presto she'd lost a pound! The interviewing Diana about the slimming was always done by Nick (Owen) and not by me, and I think after a couple of weeks she sensed that I was uneasy about this, that maybe she didn't like me, and she took me to one side and said "my dear I am an older actress with a bit of a weight problem and I would be very silly indeed to be in the same television frame as a young thing like you" and she actually said "you'll understand one day" and I do now! But she bothered to take me aside and tell me, she was very generous. What was sort of upsetting later is that by this time she was noticeably losing weight and she must have known that it was because she was ill."

26

The Big C

On September 2 1983, Diana weighed in and was on course with her weight loss. What the viewers did not see behind the warm smiling professional exterior was the fact that she was to undergo another cancer operation the following day in the Princess Margaret Hospital. In the year since her first diagnosis Diana had been undergoing treatment which included both tablets and chemotherapy. During a routine scan a trace of cancerous tissue was discovered and surgery was immediately arranged.

Alan was away in Greece filming an episode of the television series 'Hart to Hart' with Robert Wagner and Stephanie Powers when Diana called to let him have the news, telling him not to worry and that she would be fine. Alan immediately went into worried mode remembering back to 1982 and her previous operation. All flights to London from Greece were fully booked, but he knew he had to get back, even asking the American Air Force to drop him by parachute over Salisbury Plain. In the end he managed to get to Amsterdam by private jet and from there a flight to London, arriving two hours before her operation was scheduled.

The operation revealed that malignant cells had spread to Diana's stomach. The cancer had returned. She was, as always, in buoyant and positive spirits speaking to the media the next day "They operated successfully. Took away the nasty bit and found absolutely nothing else.

So, thanks be to God, I'm clear." Diana was in hospital for eight days. The doctors wanted her to remain longer, but she had promised to be home for Jason's fourteenth birthday on September 11.

On September 7 Anne Robinson of the Daily Mirror wrote "Last weekend Diana Dors was rushed to hospital for an emergency operation to remove a cancerous tumour. "I refuse to be frightened" she was announcing just as soon as the anaesthetic had worn off. A typical example of her wonderful resilience, optimism and stubborn refusal to give in when the going gets tough.

And it is the reason a fifties sex symbol has become a much loved British institution. When age called a halt to her pin-up image, she went on to make a second career as a first-rate comedienne and actress"

Further in the piece she mentioned the dieting slot concluding "Thousands of women have been helped by her dieting. Even more will be comforted by the courage she has adopted to the threat of cancer. Thank you Diana, for giving us so many years of wonderful entertainment. And I know you'll all join me in wishing her a very, very, speedy recovery."

Diana returned to her dieting slot on TVam after missing just one week's appearance. Nick Owen was sent by the show's producers to interview her at Orchard Manor on October 7. In answer to his question "Are you scared of Cancer?" She replied "Yes, Nick, of course I'm scared. I don't want it to keep coming back, but then I shall fight it all the way; it's chosen the wrong person in choosing me. But then you see, you must never let this thing get you down because it's cancer."

"My faith in God has helped me through all this. You know, I've had an awful lot of books sent to me by well-wishers about *Mind Over Cancer, Diet Over Cancer,* and all sorts of theories about what one should or should not do. Basically, yes, I'm sure they're fine and I'm thankful to the doctors and the medical technology we have today – they're wonderful people and we're living in a great age where we can fight this sort of thing – but we can only do it if we're sensible ourselves. Basically, Nick, if you really want the answer, I'm scared, of course, but I know God is protecting me, and I don't know why He is saving me, but He's done it three times now and I just know there is no way in which He will allow me to have cancer again."

On 28 October Diana weighed in for the last time and she had beaten her target. The following day a piece appeared in the Daily Mirror along with a stunning picture by Andy Hosie of her in a slim black dress, with the heading 'Diana 52 years slimmer!' and going on to say "Delighted Diana Dors was celebrating a slimming triumph yesterday. She set herself a target 17 weeks ago of losing 52lbs – one pound for each year of her life. By last Sunday her 52nd birthday, she had made it. And yesterday she was given a big party by her partners in a TV-am diet programme."

The 'slim-in' slot led to Diana being given an Agony Aunt spot on TV-am, to be called 'Open Dors' and in the same week of October 1983 she also began a column in the News of the World called 'Diana Dors …Straight from the Heart.' She wrote "Someone once said that only a fool celebrates getting a year older, and maybe they are right. But this year, one week into being 52, I really have reason to toast myself in champagne. Why? Because yet again Dors has done it. And what have I done? Survived!"

Her relationship with TV-am sadly took a downward spiral mainly because during her diet slots Diana kept promoting a 'diet calculator' that she said had helped her over the last months. The television company had held back over 3,000 letters from fans, as they wanted more information about the item, and the Independent Broadcasting Authority were consulted for advice. A court case resulted which did not resolve anything, and on 8 December 1983 a piece appeared in the Daily Mirror under the heading 'Diana calls TV-am truce' going on to say 'Slimline Diana Dors called a truce yesterday in a High Court battle with TV-am over 3,000 fan letters.

Diana claims the letters are hers. They were written by viewers asking for the diet calculator she used in her 'fight against flab' on TV-am.

The breakfast TV bosses say they are keeping the letters because Diana broke ITV rules by giving a free advertisement for the calculator in normal programme time.

Now Diana, who says she has no financial interest in the calculator, hopes the issue can be settled without a legal battle.

She said "I have apologised to TV-am if I broke any rules. We had a very good working relationship and I hope it can now get back to normal."

Diana who has lost 54lb said "They told me my show had hoisted TV-am in the ratings.

"I shall be going to work as normal this Friday. No one has told me not to."

27

The Final Days

The new year of 1984 saw both Diana and Alan busy with their careers. Diana was writing her columns, appearing on 'Open Dors' and dealing with mountains of correspondence while Alan was commuting to London appearing in commercials and doing 'voice-overs'.

In March Diana started work on what was to be her last film 'Steaming', which was adapted from Nell Dunn's stage play about a group of women who meet each week at the public baths, and share the highs and lows of life with one another. Diana played Violet the manageress who looked after everybody. The film was directed by the famous Joseph Losey.

During the filming she went into hospital for more tests and it was discovered that the cancer was now infecting her lymph glands. The doctors put her on a course of tablets which she sometimes did not take as they made her feel nauseous which meant she could not give her best for the camera.

As far as director Joseph Losey was concerned, he would not even have known she was so ill because she never gave any indication of her condition or that she merited any special treatment. One of the film crew members said "Diana was absolutely sensational. She put everything she had into it. She was on the set at 6am every day, and was never late – and she looked her best at all times. In fact, everyone kept complimenting her on how marvellous she looked."

Actress Felicity Dean who played the character of Dawn recalled "She had lost weight, and seemed in wonderful spirits. She didn't give any hint of how ill she was. She was professional as an actress and wouldn't inflict it on anyone. She would do what she had to do with a minimum of energy and then go off to her room or sit down. She never told anyone." Sarah Miles another co-star said "Diana was great fun to work with. She kept us in fits of laughter all the time, and no one knew what she was going through."

The film had only just been completed when Diana was rushed to hospital on 28 April with severe stomach pains. It was discovered that her bowel was blocked, but her doctors could not be sure that the cancer was responsible. On Monday an operation was performed to remove the blockage, but although it went well, the surgeon discovered that the cancer had spread throughout the body and informed Alan she only had a couple of weeks to live. Four days after the operation it was obvious that the end was not far off. Diana lay propped up on pillows, very tired but calm, touched by all the calls, cards and flowers she was receiving. Columnist Jean Rook wrote in the Daily Express:

'Di, a nation is praying for you, pulling for you. You're our solid "Golden Oldie", the very best of unbeatable British. You've shown more guts than they've taken away and we love you and are proud of you for what you've been for fifty-two glorious years. Our own. Bounce back, soon!'

Alan was by her side at the hospital constantly. Early on the morning of Friday 4 May 1984 he left the room for a short period while the nurses attended to Diana. When he returned he could not believe how beautiful she looked. Her blonde hair had been brushed out; she was wearing her favourite nightie and necklace with the letters D-O-R-S on it. Later that day she slipped into a coma and at 9pm passed peacefully away. Alan rang Jason at home to break the sad news and then prepared the now famous statement for the awaiting journalists "I have lost my wife and soul mate. My son has lost a friend and mother, and the world has lost a legend."

The Requiem Mass and Funeral took place at the Church of the Sacred Heart in Sunningdale on 11 May 1984. Diana was laid to rest

Diana as Violet in her final film "Steaming"

REQUIEM MASS
AND
FUNERAL SERVICE
FOR
Mrs ALAN LAKE

(Miss DIANA DORS)

CHURCH OF THE SACRED HEART
SUNNINGDALE

11th, May 1984

dressed in a gold lame evening gown with a matching cape, and the DORS necklace she had been wearing when she died. Alan wore the same pinstripe suit he had worn in court when he received his prison sentence. After the funeral he would burn it to help destroy the painful memories of the past.

The church was filled with celebrities and friends including Barbara Windsor, Freddie Starr, Lionel Blair, Danny La Rue, and Shirley Bassey. There was also Charlie Kray, mourning himself, but also representing his brothers Ronnie and Reggie. Patrick Holt from her early Rank acting days and Richard O'Sullivan who she had appeared with in television's 'Dick Turpin' in 1981. Local people who could not fit in the church were able to show their respect from outside where the service was relayed by a public address system.

Diana's favourite music was played during the service. The entry hymn was 'Dear Lord and Father of mankind'. Actor and close friend Lionel Jeffries read the lesson which was taken from 1 Corinthians 13, St Paul's poem about love. Patrick Holt said "I'm here to wish 'au revoir' to our darling Diana, a lovely girl, with all the heart and love we can give her – an 'au revoir' because I know we shall meet again. She will always be with us." He went on to read a poem which had been chosen by Alan – 'Death is Nothing At All.' A reminder that she was not far away, just in another room. 'And just because she is out of sight do not let her be out of mind. Think of her, pray for her – she is somewhere very near.' During the communion Wendy Kessach sang Handel's 'I know that my Redeemer liveth.', and the whole congregation joined for one of Diana's favourite hymns 'Amazing Grace.' Diana was laid to rest a mile away from the church in Sunningdale Cemetery. As her coffin was lowered, Alan dropped a single pink rose into the open grave whispering "I Love You."

The nations press was full of tributes to Diana the next day. A piece by Anne Robinson of the Daily Mirror headed 'Big heart behind the tinsel' went on to say "The saddest piece of news to greet me on my return was that Diana Dors had died.

She was a legend. And she deserved to be. Not just because she was so professional and talented but also because she went to enormous trouble to ensure the Press knew her side of every story.

I first heard from her after I'd sent up her TV-am diet. We'd all need housekeepers and chefs to cope with the shopping, chopping, pureeing and cooking her recipes entailed, I suggested.

She wrote me a long letter gently explaining how many women become depressed and suicidal because they are overweight. After that she was regularly in touch. We had lunch just before Christmas. A treat, she suggested to ease the burden of Christmas shopping!

As usual, she was terrific fun to be with, anxious to hear all my family news and ironically looking the picture of health after losing nearly two stone in weight.

Diana Dors never failed to put into practice the old showbiz maxim that however disastrous the odds, the show must go on.

Her uncrushable optimism, I'm glad to say, was with her till the end."

Alan took Diana's passing very badly, but initially made a strong attempt to put on a brave face to the outside world. As winter approached however many painful memories assailed him with the advent of so many anniversaries – her birthday, the anniversary of their wedding day and also of their first meeting.

In early October he was invited to a christening at the home of one of his closest friends, comedian Freddie Starr, but phoned him to say that Jason had flu and he wanted to stay with him. Talking in 1987 Freddie said "then he confessed that the depression had got too bad, and he hadn't wanted to spoil the occasion for me." Later the same day he did visit Freddie staying till 10pm in the evening. They sat together drinking coffee, but Alan seemed incapable of looking into the future.

With Diana gone and the financial drop in the family income he was now experiencing, Alan had no choice but to put Orchard Manor up for sale. It was put on the market for £325,000. With the approach of October 10, the day he and Diana had first met, his depression worsened. Jason was now working as an actor, and in a play called 'Breaking the Silence' which was in rehearsal at the Barbican. On the morning of the 10th Alan drove him to the station to catch the train to London, and then returned home where he was expecting prospective buyers to view the property. He was very restless and could not settle.

His housekeeper tried to reassure him that everything would be okay but he would not be placated. Eventually he went into his study where he spent the rest of the morning.

At around 1 o'clock he received a telephone call from journalist Jean Rook asking for a few comments about the sale of the house. Alan asked if he could put it off for a few days until things settled down a bit saying "it's a bad day today, a very bad day. It's the day I met her."

At 1.45pm Honor Webb, his housekeeper, heard a loud bang. She ran upstairs to investigate, and found Alan lying dead on the floor in Jason's bedroom. There was blood on the wall, and next to his body was a shotgun which he had put to his head only a few minutes previously. He had left no suicide note. All that was in his study were some lines written on his grey lined writing pad:

"Tick tock

Clock on the wall,

I believed in our love,

Yes – I believed it all."

A week following his death saw many of the same congregation who had attended Diana's funeral, back in the same church. Jason occupied the same place that his father had done at Diana's funeral. Any tears he shed were in private. Sitting with his back straight and head held high, he was the one left to hold everything together which he did remarkably well. Clutching his Aunt Vilma's hand as they followed Alan's coffin from the church, he retained his composure as he laid a single rose in his father's grave.

The inquest showed that Alan suffered with what we now know as a bi polar disorder, but was then known as manic depression. The family physician Dr Michael Loxton said at the time "Alan was recovering from a nervous breakdown earlier this year when Diana became mortally ill. During the last few weeks of her life, he hardly ever left her side and in the last few days hardly ever slept. Immediately after her death he was called upon to organise a very public funeral. Due to physical exhaustion caused by these events the depression returned. He was in this state of weakness and deep despair when he took his own life."

Publicity portrait from 1979

Epilogue

Diana's Lasting Legacy

The aftermath of Alan's death saw numerous articles published in both newspapers and magazines, some complementary, others defamatory, but when the dust settled, Diana was remembered with both warmth and affection by those who truly knew her and by the public in general. Diana's biographer Damon Wise writing in 1998 said 'Andy Warhol once said, with a sly ambivalence that went unnoticed, that in the future everyone would be famous for fifteen minutes.' A very profound statement as now in the twenty first century 'Celebrity' status is so often a misused description referring to people who are just famous for being famous, but with no real talent to deserve this accolade.

Damon Wise went on to say 'Diana Dors was famous for thirty-seven years with scarcely a break, and when she died, she had achieved all her possible ambitions – to be a film star, to be a singer, to be a TV personality. There was only one goal left to tackle: she wanted to be herself. In this she was successful.'

Diana was a real person, what you saw was what you got. People from all stations in society could relate to her. She was a survivor in an industry with so many pitfalls and disappointments, as well as exciting success stories. Throughout her career she was constantly compared with Marilyn Monroe, but in the end the comparisons were unfounded, as Diana would cast off the 'blonde bombshell' image, going on to carve out a very successful career as a character actress of considerable distinction, as well as a talented presenter, interviewer and writer. Above all she epitomized what the word 'star' truly means.

Today people are more aware of and interested in Diana Dors than just re-runs and DVD releases of her films would explain. Word of mouth, from generation to generation must be what accounts for it, and that, after all is how legends are made.

Diana As Cabaret Artiste

Diana enjoyed a very successful career as a Cabaret Artiste during the 1950s through to the 1980s both in Britain and overseas. During the 1950s many of her engagements in the United Kingdom were at theatres which came under the Moss Empires/ Stoll Moss banner.

I am indebted to Keith of Alexander's Theatre Emporium for putting at my disposal some original reports of a number of Diana's appearances in various parts of the country. These reports were on cards, and Keith supplied me with the following information on these:-

"A unique and interesting piece of theatre history. These large index cards have come from the Moss Empires/Stoll Moss archive, where a file was kept on each performer/show appearing on their circuit, which included the London Palladium and some of the most famous theatres across the country.

The information seemed to have been updated after each appearance. I am not sure whether the cards were sent across the country for the various managers to complete and then kept in HQ or whether the managers sent or phoned in their comments and the cards updated in the central office.

The information included the theatre name, date of the appearance, how the act was received by the audience and mini reviews by the manager. It also includes specific figures about salaries and grosses. Also if anything out of the ordinary occurred. Some of the comments could be quite candid. A fascinating insight into the variety world."

I make no apologies for grammatical errors as I have copied these reports exactly as they appear on the cards.

HALL	DATE	MANAGER'S REPORT	RETURN	SALARY	ESTIMATED VALUE 1.	2.
		Collins				
		DIANA DORS.				
B.TON	7.6.54	Following the strong act of Authors & Swinson. With Miss Williams permission these two acts were switched for the second house and she did very much better. Her material is not very strong and unless the act improves a great deal I feel that she will keep people out of the Theatre rather than bring them in at a future booking. However, this week her name is definitely drawing a certain number of people but she is receiving adverse comments so the patrons are coming out.	No unless will change	87 £am £150	75	75
NOTTS.E	28.6.54	Very well received. A competent artiste with a most attractive appearance to assist. Splendid personality and doing well with material that is just fair.	Yes	FRANKIE VAUGHAN 125	125	
Rham	4.8.58	Received excellently. Presents a first class act. Has a wonderful personality & has gone to considerable trouble to present the act with style and taste Press reports are first class	6/10	60/0	£560	230

Brighton Hippodrome 7.6.54

-following the strong act of Authors & Swinson. With Miss Williams permission these two acts were switched for the second house and she did very much better. Her material is not very strong and unless the act improves a great deal I feel that she will keep people out of the theatre rather than bring them in at a future booking. However, this week is definitely drawing a certain number of people but she is receiving adverse comments as the patrons are coming out.

Nottingham Empire 28.6.54

Very well received. A competent artist with a most attractive appearance to assist. Splendid personality and doing well with material that is just fair.

Birmingham Hippodrome 4.8.58

Received excellently. Presents a first class act. Has a wonderful personality & has gone to considerable trouble to present the act with style and taste. Press reports are first class.

Bristol Hippodrome 18.8.58

This artiste of course needs no introduction and there is no doubt that she is a very talented young lady. Glamorous, with a warm and pleasing personality, her act appealed. She was given vocal assistance by the Group One Quartet and her gagging partner Dickie Dawson. Her fabulous dresses brought forth great admiration.

Manchester Palace 8.9.58

Very good reception. The act she does is merely? A means of bringing the "Dors" aura in the flesh to the public & she achieves this object very creditably if not in the glamorous environment one might wish. Her act is pleasant enough without being talented in any respect what more could be expected. She sings nicely, puts over a good point number & does some patter which however is the least successful of her attainments.

Liverpool Empire 29. 9.58

Received very well indeed. An accomplished performer presents a bright and entertaining act to very good audience reaction.

Finsbury Park Empire 6.10.58

Very good reception. Entertainment of a quality which surprises the curious of a striking but artificial appearance. She talks exceedingly well good diction with Vocals and is quite successful with comedy. Her best work comes in her business with Dickie Dawson. Confident patter and an interesting vocal.

Bristol 13.10.58

Very well received. Miss Dors has charm and a good personality. She puts over her songs very well and her voice suits the type of songs she sings but the cross talk with Dickie Dawson lacks the essential humour, this being due to the inexperience of Mr Dawson. Her costumes are very extravagant and are a must in an act of this sort. Her opening costume causes a flutter of laughter to go through the audience. This of course may be her intention.

Chiswick Empire 20.10.58

Introduced in song by Group One. Is revealed in a most striking costume creation. While one would not call her a "singer", she puts over a 35 minute act which is good entertainment, which includes songs – original about herself and popular – comedy patter and impressions of how Yorkshire – Scottish Irish & Welsh would put over a nursery rhyme. Before the finale she is joined again by Group One and also Dickie Dawson joins her in some gagging. Took a very good curtain.

Book Bibliography

Listed in Author order

Connecting Dors
The Legacy of Diana Dors
Niema Ash (in collaboration with Jason Dors-Lake)
    Purple Inc Press 2011
Diana Dors
Tony Bilbow
    Channel 4 Television 1990
Diana Dors Hurricane in Mink
David Bret
    JR Books 2010
Swingin' Dors
Diana Dors
    World Distributors. 1960
For Adults Only
Diana Dors
(Associate Editor : Jack Hobbs)
    W H Allen 1978
    Star Book (Paperback Division of W H Allen & Co Ltd) 1978
Behind Closed Dors
Diana Dors
(Associate Editor : Jack Hobbs)
    W.H. Allen 1979

Star Book (Paperback Division of W H Allen & Co Ltd) 1979
Dors by Diana
Diana Dors
 Queen Anne Press 1981
 Futura Publications 1981
Diana Dors' A-Z of Men
Diana Dors
 Macdonald & Co Ltd 1984
 Futura Publications 1984
Diana Dors Only A Whisper Away
Joan Flory and Damien Walne
 Lennard Publishing 1987
 Cassell Illustrated 1988
 Chivers Press 1988
Come By Sunday
The Fabulous Ruined Life of Diana Dors
Damon Wise
 Sidgwick & Jackson 1998
 Pan Books 1999
 Charnwood 1999

Bibliography

Selected magazine and newspaper articles consulted
Listed by date of Publication

Introducing Diana Dors, What's On in London, January 31 1947

In The News, Theatre World, March 1950

Remains to Be Seen, Theatre by Kenneth A Hurren, What's On In London, December 26 1952

The Great Game, Preview by Maud Hughes, Picture Show & Film Pictorial, May 9 1953

Is Your Honeymoon Really Necessary? The New Films reviewed by F. Maurice Speed, What's On In London, September 25 1953

Intimately Yours, Diana Dors, Tit-Bits, 24 October 1953

Intimately Yours, Diana Dors, Tit-Bits, 31 October 1953

Value For Money, ShowGirl Glamour Review, Vol 1 No 6 1955

The Trials of Diana Dors, Robert Muller, Picture Post, 22 January 1955

Siren From Swindon, Kenneth Tynan, Everybody's, March 12 1955

The Remarkable Diary of Diana Dors, Margaret Hinxman, Picturegoer, May 7 1955

A Kid For Two Farthings, The Cinema by F. Maurice Speed, What's On in London, May 13 1955

Round the British Studios, Picture Show & Film Pictorial August 20 1955

Out of Dors, Diana Dors, Picturegoer, February 25 1956

I Can't for ever be a Glamour Bombshell, Diana Dors, Picturegoer, April 14 1956

Diana – Queen of Cannes, Robert Muller, Picture Post, 19 May 1956

Diana Goes to Work, Charles Hamblett, Picture Post, August 18 1956

Girls, You'll go crazy over him, Diana Dors, Picturegoer, August 25 1956

In the Lap of Luxury, Diana Dors, Picturegoer, September 1 1956

They want me as the Blonde Bombshell, Out of Dors in Hollywood …, Picturegoer, September 29 1956

Dennis, Hollywood and Me, Charles Kirschner, Picturegoer, January 5 1957

These Dors rumours are baloney, Elizabeth Forrest, Picturegoer, February 22 1958

The Lady goes Straight, Diana Dors at Chichester, by Ian Woodward, Woman's Journal, June 1974

Oedipus Tyrannus, Peter Ansorge, Plays and Players, August 1974

Who 'Pinched' Diana's Bottom?, Brian Wasley, The Sun, Thursday June 26 1975

A Boadicea for the 20th Century, Clive Limpkin, The Sunday Times, January 17 1982

To lose Diana would be like losing my soul, Derek Bromfield, Woman's Own, January 14 1984

Diana Dors Dead, Tony Bassett & Peter Bond, The Sun, May 5 1984

A Legend to the very end, Diana's bravest performance, Suzanne Thomas, Woman, June 2 1984

Diana Dors' Husband : His last words, Jean Rook, Daily Express, Thursday October 11 1984

I Can't live without her, Roger Beam and Edward Laxton, Daily Mirror, October 11 1984

Diana Dors Part One, Ken Roche, TV Times, 13 – 19 October 1984

Courage of Orphan Jason, Paul Callan, Daily Mirror, Thursday October 18 1984

Diana Dors Part Two, Ken Roche, TV Times, 20 – 26 October 1984

Diana Dors Part Three, Jane Ennis, TV Times, 27 October – 2 November 1984

"Exuding 100 per cent pure sex" : Diana Dors and Is Your Honeymoon

Really Necessary, Vic Pratt, British Film Institute 2010

That Diana Dors Moment, Damon Wise, British Film Institute 2010

Diana Dors, My Mother, Jason Lake, British Film Institute 2010

Deep End, David Thompson, British Film Institute 2011

Permissive British Cinema?, Yvonne Tasker, British Film Institute 2011

Murder. Mystery and Missing Scenes : Miss Tulip Stays the Night, Vic Pratt, British Film Institute 2011

Diana Dors : The Hollywood Dream Draws Nearer, Huw Prall, British Film Institute 2011

Knock Me Down With a Centre Forward : The Great Game, Vic Pratt, British Film Institute 2011

Clothes Maketh the Woman : Diana Dors' Style in the Adelphi Films, Jenny Hammerton, British Film Institute 2011

Cinemagic – Diana Dors, Alana Duffy, Evergreen, Summer 2012

Swinging Dors, Huw Prall, Best of British Past and Present, October 2012

Cannes in the Fifties, Ben Machell, The Times Magazine, 18 May 2013

The British Bombshell : The story of Diana Dors, Huw Prall, Vintage & Homemade Living, Issue Seven, 2013

The Happy Family, Huw Prall, Vintage & Homemade Living Issue Nine 2013

Goddess from Swindon, Huw Prall, His Vintage Life, September 2013

The Siren from Swindon, Huw Prall, The People's Friend, December 13 2014

Filmography

THE SHOP AT SLY CORNER (1946)
(USA : The Code of Scotland Yard)

Director & Producer : George King. Screenplay : Katherine Strueby from the play by Edward Percy. Photography : Hone Glendinning. Production Company : Pennant Pictures/London Films. Distributor : British Lion. 92 minutes. Cert A.

Heiss (Oskar Homolka), a London antique dealer, is in fact a convict escaped from Devil's Island, a secret shared only by his partner Morris (Manning Whiley) and hidden from his violinist daughter Margaret (Muriel Pavlow). His assistant Archie (Kenneth Griffith) finds out and blackmails him. Heiss and Morris kill Archie, but Morris dies in a car crash. Cornered by police, Heiss commits suicide on the night of Margaret's concert debut.

Rest of Cast : Derek Farr. Kathleen Harrison. Garry Marsh. Irene Handl. Johnnie Schofield. Diana Dors. Jan von Loewen.

HOLIDAY CAMP (1947)

Director : Ken Annakin. Producer : Sydney Box. Screenplay : Sydney Box, Peter Rogers, Mabel Constanduros, Denis Constanduros, Ted Willis. Photography : Jack Cox. Production Company : Gainsborough. Distributor : General Film Distributors. 97 minutes. Cert A.

Stories of characters in a holiday camp: a bus driver and his wife, young son and war-widowed daughter, a sailor who has been jilted; a homicidal maniac posing as an RAF officer, a spinster taking a holiday after years of devotion to her invalid mother, a man-chasing-waitress; two card-sharps; a composer and the girl he can't marry because of family opposition. Some find romance, but the waitress finds death at the hands of the 'mannequin muderer' who is caught by police.

Cast : Jack Warner. Kathleen Harrison. Flora Robson. Dennis Price. Hazel Court. Emrys Jones. Esma Cannon. Yvonne Owen. Esmond Knight. Jimmy Hanley. Peter Hammond. John Blythe. Dennis Harkin. Beatrice Varley. Jeannette Tregarthen. Susan Shaw. Maurice Denham. Jane Hylton. Jack Raine. Alfie Bass. Patricia Roc. Reginald Purdell. Diana Dors. Gerry Wilmott. Charlie Chester. Pamela Braman. John Stone. Phil Fowler. Jack Ellis.

DANCING WITH CRIME (1947)

Director : John Paddy Carstairs. Producer : James Carter. Screenplay : Brock Williams. Photography : Reginald Wyer. Production Company : Coronet/Alliance. Distributor : Paramount. 83 minutes. Cert A.

Ted Peters (Richard Attenborough), a young taxi-driver recently demobbed, nearly gets mixed up with a gang of crooks, then one night finds the body of the ringleader Dave Robinson (Bill Owen), an ex-army pal, in his taxi. With the help of his girlfriend Joy (Sheila Sim), Ted tracks down the murderer, a slimy black marketeer (Barry K. Barnes). even though it places his own life in danger.

Rest of Cast : Garry Marsh. John Warwick. Judy Kelly. Barry Jones. Cyril Chamberlain. John Salew. Hamish Menzies. Peter Croft. Norman Shelley. Dennis Wyndham. Diana Dors. Patricia Dainton. Dirk Bogarde. Johnnie Schofield.

STREETS PAVED WITH WATER (1947)

Director : Joe Mendoza. Anthony Skene. Producer : Sydney Box. Screenplay : Joe Mendoza. Anthony Skene. Photography : Stephen Dade. Production Company : Gainsborough.

Cast : Maxwell Reed. Jane Hylton. Andrew Crawford. Diana Dors. The film was never completed.

MY SISTER AND I (1948)

Director : Harold Huth. Producer : Harold Huth, John Corfield. Screenplay : A.R. Rawlinson, Joan Rees, Michael Medwin, Robert Westerby, from a novel by Emery Bonnet. Photography : Harry Waxman. Production Company : Burnham. Distributor : General Film Distributors. 97 minutes. Cert A.

Robina (Sally Ann Howes), a set designer, finds lodgings with wealthy Mrs Camelot (Martita Hunt), who owns the local theatre and takes a shine to Robina. When Mrs Camelot is murdered, suspicion falls on Robina, who is left all her money. But the revelation that Mrs Camelot's adored dead husband was not a paragon of virtue leads to the discovery of the real killer.

Rest of Cast : Barbara Mullen. Dermot Walsh. Hazel Court. Patrick Holt. Jane Hylton. Michael Medwin. Diana Dors. Stewart Rome. Joan Rees. Helen Goss. Hugh Miller. James Knight. Ian Wilson. Rory McDermott. Niall Lawlor. Elizabeth Sydney. Olwen Brookes. Jack Vyvyan. Wilfred Caithness. John Miller. Amy Dalby. Barbara Leake.

PENNY AND THE POWNALL CASE (1948)

Director : Slim Hand. Producer : John Corfield. Screenplay : William Fairchild. Photography : Jimmy Harvey. Production Company : Production Facilities. Distributor : General Film Distributors. 47 minutes. Cert A.

Model Penny (Peggy Evans) is a keen amateur 'tec. Learning that Pownall, a secret serviceman, has been murdered, she goes to Spain, scene of the crime. She is accompanied by her boss, Blair (Christopher Lee), whom she discovers to be a traitor working for the escape of Nazi war criminals. Aided by Inspector Carson (Ralph Michael), she exposes Blair's network and unmasks Pownall's killer.

Rest of Cast: Diana Dors. Frederick Piper. Olaf Pooley. Ethel Coleridge. Sam Costa. Dennis Vance. Duncan Carse. Shaun Noble. Philip Saville. John Lorrell. Peter Madden.

OLIVER TWIST (1948)

Director : David Lean. Producer : Anthony Havelock-Allan. Screenplay : David Lean, Stanley Haynes from the novel by Charles Dickens. Photography : Guy Green. Production Company : Cineguild. Distributor : General Film Distributors. 116 minutes. Cert A.

Son of a girl who dies in childbirth, young Oliver (John Howard Davies) suffers the cruel discipline of a parish workhouse in the early 1800s. He runs away from his sadistic first employer, an undertaker, and falls in with a gang of pickpockets, led by Fagin (Alec Guinness). When he is found to be the son of a rich man, the relative he will disinherit pays Fagin to have a man kill him It turns out to be murderous Bill Sykes (Robert Newton) who strangles his kind-hearted mistress Nancy (Kay Walsh), but fails to despatch Oliver, falling to his death in a rooftop chase with police. Fagin goes to the gallows and Oliver starts a new life.

Rest of Cast : Francis L. Sullivan. Henry Stephenson. Mary Clare. Anthony Newley. Ralph Truman. Josephine Stuart. Kathleen Harrison. Gibb McLaughlin. Amy Veness. Diana Dors. Frederick Lloyd. Maurice Denham. W.G. Fay. Henry Edwards. Hattie Jacques. Betty Paul. Ivor Barnard. Deidre Doyle. Edie Martin. Fay Middleton. Michael Dear. Graveley Edwards. Peter Bull. John Potter. Maurice Jones. Kenneth Downey.

GOOD TIME GIRL (1948)

Director : David Macdonald. Producer : Sydney Box, Samuel Goldwyn Jr. Screenplay : Sydney Box, Muriel Box, Ted Willis, from a novel by

Arthur la Bern. Photography : Stephen Dade. Production Company : Triton. Distributor : General Film Distributors. 93 minutes. Cert A.

Caught stealing, Gwen (Jean Kent) is sacked by her boss and beaten by her father. She is found a job in a nighclub, where the owner Max (Herbert Lom) takes her under his wing. One of his waiters Jimmy (Peter Glenville), gets her to pawn stolen jewellery. She is arrested in the flat of a friend, Red (Dennis Price). Sent to a reformatory, she escapes and gets to Brighton, becoming the mistress of Danny, a racketeer (Griffith Jones). After a car smash in which a policeman dies, Gwen breaks with him and ends up with two GI deserters. In a holdup, they shoot a man – Red. For her involvement, Gwen gets 15 years.

Rest of Cast : Flora Robson. Bonar Colleano. Hugh McDermott. Nora Swinburne. Elwyn Brook-Jones. Jill Balcon. Beatrice Varley. Margaret Barton. Garry Marsh. John Blythe. Diana Dors. George Carney. Any Veness. Zena Marshall. Harry Ross. Orlando Martins. Jack Raine. Michael Hordern. George Merritt. Renee Gadd. Joan Young. Phyllis Stanley. Betty Nelson. Danny Green.

THE CALENDAR (1948)

Director : Arthur Crabtree. Producer : Anthony Darnborough. Screenplay : Geoffrey Kerr, from the play by Edgar Wallace. Photography : Reginald Wyer. Production Company : Gainsborough. Distributor : General Film Distributors. 80 minutes. Cert A.

Garry Anson's (John McCallum) fiancée Wenda (Greta Gynt) leaves him when he loses all his money horse-racing. While drunk, a depressed Garry agrees to "pull" one of his horses. He sends Wenda a telegram asking her not to back it. Sober, he changes his mind, revoking the 'gram on the back of £100 note. Wenda refuses to back him at a stewards' inquiry, but his trainer Mollie (Sonia Holm) burgles Wenda's safe, and tricks her into admitting the truth.

Rest of Cast : Raymond Lovell. Leslie Dwyer. Charles Victor. Barry Jones. Felix Aylmer. Sydney King. Diana Dors. Fred Payne. Noel Howlett. Claude Bailey. Desmond Roberts. Cyril Chamberlain. O.B. Clarence. Constance Smith.

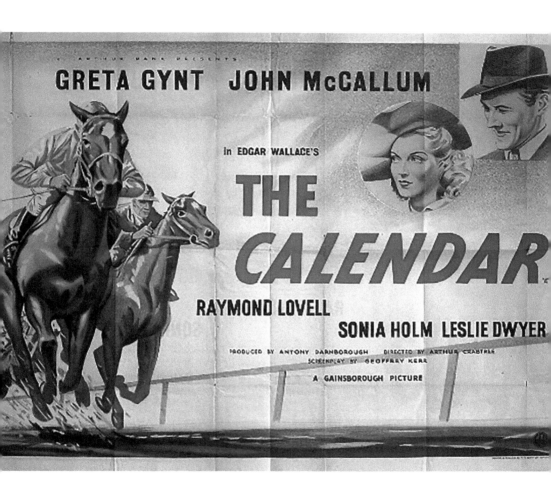

HERE COME THE HUGGETTS (1948)

Director : Ken Annakin. Producer : Betty Box. Screenplay : Mabel and Denis Constanduros, Muriel and Sydney Box, Peter Rogers. Photography : Reg Wyer. Production Company : Gainsborough. Distributor : General Film Distributors. 93 minutes. Cert A.

Their glamorous blonde relation Diana (Diana Dors) upsets the Huggetts' well-ordered household and nearly loses father Joe (Jack Warner) his job. After spending seven days in jail following a crash in the family car, Diana leaves. Other problems, mostly romantic, are also solved.

Rest of Cast : Kathleen Harrison. Jane Hylton. Susan Shaw. Petula Clark. Jimmy Hanley. David Tomlinson. Peter Hammond. John Blythe. Amy Veness. Clive Morton. Maurice Denham. Doris Hare. Dandy Nichols. Hal Osmond. Esma Cannon.

VOTE FOR HUGGETT (1948)

Director : Ken Annakin. Producer : Betty Box. Screenplay : Mabel and Denis Constanduros, Allan Mackinnon. Photography : Reginald Wyer. Production Company : Gainsborough. Distributor : General Film Distributors. 84 minutes. Cert A.

Up for election as borough councillor, Joe Huggett (Jack Warner) suggests a new lido as a war memorial. A suitable site is part-owned by his wife (Kathleen Harrison). She refuses to sell, but her niece Diana (Diana Dors) forges her signature, and Joe is in hot water. Luckily his daughter Susan (Susan Shaw) discovers the forgery and all ends well, with Joe winning the election.

Rest of Cast : Petula Clark. David Tomlinson. Peter Hammond. Amy Veness. Hubert Gregg. John Blythe. Anthony Newley. Charles Victor. Adrianne Allen. Frederick Piper. Eliot Makeham. Clive Morton. Norman Shelley. Lyn Evans. Hal Osmond. Elizabeth Hunt. Empsie Bowman. Isa Bowman. Nellie Bowman. Ferdy Mayne.

With John Blythe in "Vote for Huggett"

IT'S NOT CRICKET (1948)

Director : Alfred Roome, Roy Rich. Producer : Betty Box. Screenplay : Bernard McNab, Gerard Bryant, Lyn Lockwood. Photography : Gordon Lang. Production Company : Gainsborough. Distributor : General Film Distributors. 77 minutes. Cert U.

For letting a dangerous Nazi (Maurice Denham) escape, Major Bright (Basil Radford) and Captain Early (Naunton Wayne) are 'retired' from the army. They set up as private detectives, but the Nazi still dogs their tracks, popping up in every case and finally involving them in a lunatic cricket match where the ball contains a stolen diamond.

Rest of Cast : Susan Shaw. Alan Wheatley. Nigel Buchanan. Jane Carr. Leslie Dwyer. Diana Dors. Patrick Waddington. Edward Lexy. Frederick Piper. Mary Hinton. Margaret Withers. Brian Oulton. Cyril Chamberlain. Charles Cullum. John Mann. Hal Osmond. Sheila Huntington. John Warren. Viola Lyel. Arthur Hambling. Hamilton Keene. Meinhart Maur. John Boxer.

A BOY, A GIRL AND A BIKE (1949)

Director : Ralph Smart. Producer : Ralph Keene. Screenplay : Ted Willis. Photography : Ray Elton. Production Company : Gainsborough. Distributor : General Film Distributors. 92 minutes. Cert U.

Sam and Susie (Patrick Holt, Honor Blackman) belong to a Yorkshire cycling club. David (John McCallum), a rich boy who, like Sam, fancies Susie, joins to be near her and stays to help the club win an important race. A bicycle thief is chased and caught; Sam wins Susie; and veteran secretary Steve (Leslie Dwyer) pairs up with the lady (Megs Jenkins) who runs the 'club café'.

Rest of Cast : Diana Dors. Anthony Newley. John Blythe. Margaret Avery. Barry Letts. Thora Hird. Maurice Denham. Alison Leggatt. Julien Mitchell. Amy Veness. Hal Osmond. Cyril Chamberlain. Vera Cook. Joan Seton. Lyn Evans. Margot Bourke. Dnnis Peck. Vera Williams. Geoffrey Best. John Howlett. Jennifer Jayne. Patrick Halstead.

DIAMOND CITY (1949)

Director : David Macdonald. Producer : A. Frank Bundy. Screenplay : Roger Bray, Roland Pertwee. Photography : Reginald Wyer. Production Company : Gainsborough. Distributor : General Film Distributors. 90 minutes. Cert U.

The opening of the South African diamond fields in the 1870s brings a flood of illicit diamond buyers. A diggers' community is formed in Klipdrift, where Parker (David Farrar), a tough adventurer, gets a concession for mining ahead of Muller (Niall MacGinnis), an unscrupulous rum trader. The rivalry between them leads to bloodshed and a republic is proclaimed before the British government takes over.

Rest of Cast : Honor Blackman. Diana Dors. Andrew Crawford. Marvyn Johns. Phyllis Monkman. Bill Owen. Philo Hauser. Hal Osmond. John Blythe. Reginald Tate. Ronald Adam. Dennis Vance. Norris Smith. John Salew. Tony Quinn. Slim Harris. Julian Somers. Harry Quashie. Arthur Lane. John Warren. Ernest Butcher.

DANCE HALL (1950)

Director : Charles Crichton. (Associate) Producer : E. V. H. Emmett. Screenplay : E. V. H. Emmett, Diana Morgan, Alexander Mackendrick. Photography : Douglas Slocombe. Production Company : Ealing Studios. Distributor : General Film Distributors. 80 mins. Cert A.

Four factory girls (Natasha Parry, Petula Clark, Diana Dors, Jane Hylton) let their hair down on the floor of the local palais de danse on weekend evenings. Two find romance there, two enter a competition. Eve (Natasha Parry) is attracted by a smoothie (Bonar Colleano), with whom she enters the contest, but eventually goes back to Phil (Donald Houston) her old boyfriend.

Rest of Cast : Sydney Tafler. Douglas Barr. Gladys Henson. Fred Johnson. James Carney. Kay Kendall. Eunice Gayson. Hy Hazell. Dandy Nichols. Grace Arnold. Thomas Heathcote. Harold Goodwin. Christopher Kane. Tonie Macmillan. Alec Finter. Doris Hare. Michael Trubshawe. Geraldo and His Orchestra. Ted Heath and His Music. Wally Fryer and Margaret Barnes.

Diana, Natasha Parry, Jane Hylton, and Petula Clark in "Dance Hall"

WORM'S EYE VIEW (1951)

Director : Jack Raymond. Producer : Henry Halstead. Screenplay : R. F. Delderfield, Jack Marks, from R. F. Delderfield's play. Photography : James Wilson. Production Company : Byron. Distributor : Associated British. 77 mins. Cert U.

Events in the lives of five RAF men billeted in a suburban household during World War II. Led by Porter (Ronald Shiner), a malingering 'spiv' always on the make, the quintet plagues the life out of the vinegary landlady (Eveley Gregg), her henpecked husband, objectionable stepson and pretty daughter, to say nothing of the saucy maid (Diana Dors).

Rest of Cast : Garry Marsh. John Blythe. Bruce Seton. Digby Wolfe. Eric Davies. Christina Forrest. William Percy. Jonathan Field.

LADY GODIVA RIDES AGAIN (1951)
(USA : Bikini Baby)

Director : Frank Launder. Producer : Frank Launder, Sidney Gilliat. Screenplay : Frank Launder, Val Valentine. Photography : Wilkie Cooper. Production Company : London Films. Distributor : British Lion. 90 mins. Cert U.

Marjorie (Pauline Stroud), a pretty waitress, enters a 'Lady Godiva' beauty contest and, much to her surprise, wins. She is persuaded to enter a big beauty contest, which is fixed in her favour. Marjorie now has dreams of becoming a film star, but her contract is scrapped after she is innocently involved in a minor scandal. She ends up as a nude in a vaudeville show, but is rescued by her family, and the Australian (John McCallum) who loves her.

Rest of Cast : Dennis Price. Stanley Holloway. Gladys Henson. George Cole. Diana Dors. Bernadette O'Farrell. Kay Kendall. Eddie Byrne. Renee Houston. Dora Bryan. Alastair Sim. Sidney James. Dagmar (Dana) Wynter. Tommy Duggan. Eddie Leslie. Walford Hyden. Lisa Lee. Lyn Evans. Edward Forsyth. Peter Martyn. Fred Berger. Henry Longhurst. Felix Felton. Arthur Brander. Sidney Vivian. Arthur Howard.

John Blythe as Duke, Diana as Thelma and Ronald Shiner as Sam Porter

Clive Baxter. Paul Connell. John Harvey. Tom Gill. Rowena Gregory. Michael Ripper. Charlotte Mitchell. Toke Townley. Patricia Goddard. Richard Wattis. Googie Withers. Trevor Howard. Myrette Morven. Leslie Mitchell. Russell Waters. Joan Collins. Violet Pretty (Anne Heywood). Jimmy Young. Greta Gray. Dorothy Hocking. Madeleine Mona. Dawn Chapple. Deirdre de Peyer. Rita Wheatley. June Charlier. Simone Silva. June Hart. Maureen O'Neill. Sylvia Wren. Kismet Shahani. Marlene Ann Dee. Suzanne Levesi. Ann Hanslip. Diana Russell. Gina Egan. Evelyn Buyers. Johnnie Johnston. Enid Smeedon. Phyllis Garnett. Noel Scott-Gorman. Peter O'Farrell. Cyril Chamberlain. Syd Dean and His Band.

THE LAST PAGE (1952)
(USA : Man Bait)

Director : Terence Fisher. Producer : Anthony Hinds. Screenplay : Frederic Knott, from the play by James Hadley Chase. Photography : Walter Harvey. Production Company : Hammer / Lippert. Distributor : Exclusive. 84 mins. Cert A.

Shop assistant Ruby (Diana Dors) is convinced by her lover Jeff (Peter Reynolds) that a mild flirtation with her boss Harman (George Brent) presents a chance for blackmail. When Harman ignores the threat, Ruby's letter to his invalid wife (Isabel Dean) brings about her death. Harman pays up, Jeff accidentally kills Ruby for the money, and Harman is suspected, thanks to his jealous under-manager (Raymond Huntley). His assistant (Marguerite Chapman) tracks Jeff down, and police are just in time to prevent him strangling her.

Rest of Cast : Eleanor Summerfield. Meredith Edwards. Harry Fowler. Conrad Phillips. Lawrence Ward. Nelly Arno. David Keir. Eleanor Brown. Jack Faint. John Mann. Harold Goodwin. Archie Duncan. Cyril Saxon. Leslie Weston. Lawrence O'Madden. Ian Wilson.

MY WIFE'S LODGER (1952)

Director : Maurice Elvey. Producer : David Dent. Screenplay : Dominic

Roche, Stafford Dickens, from Dominic Roche's play. Photography : Len Harris. Production Company : Advance. Distributor : Adelphi. 80 mins. Cert A.

Willie (Dominic Roche) returns home after six years' overseas service in the army to find his house in an uproar and a lodger firmly installed. He goes out and gets drunk, but later learns from Tex, an American, that he has inherited a ranch in Texas. The lodger is revealed to be a crook and kicked out, and Willie is master in his own home.

Rest of Cast : Diana Dors. Leslie Dwyer. Olive Sloane. Alan Sedgwick. Vincent Downing. Vi Kaley.

THE GREAT GAME (1952)

Director : Maurice Elvey. Producer : David Dent. Screenplay : Wolfgang Wilhelm, from a play by Basil Thomas. Photography : Phil Grindrod. Production Company : Advance. Distributor : Adelphi. 80 mins. Cert U.

Joe Lawson (James Hayter), grasping chairman of football team Burnville United, cares little about the happiness and welfare of his players as long as relegation is avoided. His crooked deals to buy a new striker are found out, and he is forced to resign, returning to the printing business he has neglected, to find it has gone to the dogs.

Rest of Cast : Diana Dors. Thora Hird. Sheila Shand Gibbs. John Laurie. Glyn Houston. Geoffrey Toone. Jack Lambert. Meredith Edwards. Alexander Gauge. Frank Pettingell. Glenn Melvyn. Roddy Hughes. Sydney Vivian. Charles Leno. Tommy Lawton. Brentford Football Club.

THE SAINT'S RETURN (1953)
(USA : The Saint's Girl Friday)

Director : Seymour Friedman. Producer : Anthony Hinds. Screenplay: Allan Mackinnon. Photography : Walter Harvey. Production Company: Hammer. Distributor : Exclusive. 73 mins. Cert U.

American sleuth Simon Templar (Louis Hayward) alias 'The Saint', comes to England after a telegram for help from an old friend. On arrival, he discovers she has been killed in an 'accident' and decides to investigate the shady waterfront gambling crowd with which she was mixed up. He succeeds in unmasking an evil blackmailer behind a gang of gambling racketeers.

Rest of Cast : Naomi Chance. Sydney Tafler. Charles Victor. Harold Lang. Thomas Gallagher. Jane Carr. Fred Johnson. Russell Enoch (William Russell). Ian Fleming. John Wynn. Russell Napier. George Margo. Johnnie Schofield. Diana Dors.

Diana as Lulu Smith, Sheila Shand Gibbs as Mavis Pink
and Glyn Houston as Ned Rutter

IS YOUR HONEYMOON REALLY NECESSARY? (1953)

Director : Maurice Elvey. Producer : David Dent. Screenplay : Talbot Rothwell, from the play by E.V. Tidmarsh. Photography : Phil Grindrod. Production Company : Advance. Distributor : Adelphi. 79 minutes. Cert U.

An American airman (Bonar Colleano) comes to England with his bride (Diana Decker), to be met by his first wife (Diana Dors), not merely claiming alimony, but sowing seeds of doubt as to whether their divorce was valid. After numerous complications, the airman sorts it out, only to be confronted by a new candidate for his affections…

Rest of Cast : David Tomlinson. Sidney James. MacDonald Parke. Audrey Freeman.

IT'S A GRAND LIFE (1953)

Director : John E. Blakeley. Producer : John E. Blakeley. Screenplay : H. F. Maltby, Frank Randle. Photography : Ernest Palmer. Production Company : Film Studios Manchester. Distributor : Mancunian. 102 minutes. Cert U.

Accident-prone Private Randle (Frank Randle) can't even make a success of making the tea for his army unit – but he does succeed in saving a comely corporal (Diana Dors) from the lecherous clutches of his sergeant-major, and steers her into the arms of the private soldier who really loves her.

Rest of Cast : Dan Young. Michael Brennan. Jennifer Jayne. John Blythe. Anthony Hulme. Charles Peters. Arthur White. Ian Fleming. Ruth Taylor. Winifred Atwell. Jack Pye.

Diana as Candy Markham in "Is Your Honeymoon Really Necessary?"

THE WEAK AND WICKED (1953)
(USA : Young and Willing)

Director : J. Lee Thompson. Producer : Victor Skutezky. Screenplay : J. Lee Thompson, Anne Burnaby, Joan Henry, from Henry's book Who Lie in Gaol. Photography : Gilbert Taylor. Production Company : Associated British / Marble Arch. Distributor : Associated British – Pathe. 88 mins. Cert A.

Her huge gambling debts land Jean (Glynis Johns) in jail for 12 months. She meets Betty (Diana Dors), a good–time girl 'taking the rap' for a boyfriend, Babs (Jane Hylton) whose heedlessness had caused her child's death, Nellie (Olive Sloane), a shoplifter, and later Millie (Athene Seyler), a genteel old lady doing time on a trumped-up blackmail charge. On an evening out just before her release, Jean thinks Betty has absconded – but she returns, like the man (John Gregson) Jean thought she had lost.

Rest of Cast : Sidney James. Sybil Thorndike. A.E. Matthews. Anthony Nicholls. Barbara Couper. Joyce Heron. Ursula Howells. Mary Merrall. Rachel Roberts. Marjorie Rhodes. Simone Silva. Josephine Griffin. Josephine Stuart. Bessie Love. Sandra Dorne. Edwin Styles. Cecil Trouncer. Paul Carpenter. Eliot Makeham. Joan Haythorne. Jean Taylor-Smith. Thea Gregory. Tom Gill. Irene Handl. Marjorie Stewart. Hannah Watt. Kathleen Michael. Maureen Pryor. Ruth Denning. Margaret Diamond.

AS LONG AS THEY'RE HAPPY (1955)

Director : J. Lee Thompson. Producer : Raymond Stross. Screenplay : Alan Melville, from the play by Vernon Sylvaine. Photography : Gilbert Taylor. Production Company : Raymond Stross / Group. Distributor : General Film Distributors. Eastman Colour. 91 mins. Cert U.

When an American crooner (Jerry Wayne) stays at a British home, the three daughters of the house (Janette Scott, Jean(nie) Carson, Susan Stephen) go wild – so does father (Jack Buchanan), but in a different way. In the end, though, the singer is responsible for reuniting father and mother, as well as revealing the secret of his 'crying-crooner' technique – a hidden onion.

Rest of Cast : Brenda de Banzie. Diana Dors. Hugh McDermott. Nigel Green. Athene Seyler. David Hurst. Gilbert Harding. Joan Sims. Dora Bryan. Charles Hawtrey. Joan Hickson. Leslie Phillips. Jean Aubrey. Edie Martin. Susan Lyall-Grant. Peter Illing. Arnold Bell. Pauline Winter. Hattie Jaccques. Vivienne Martin. Charles Ross. Ronnie Stevens. John Blythe. Bill Shine. Norman Wisdom.

MISS TULIP STAYS THE NIGHT (1955)
(USA : Dead by Morning)

Director : Leslie Arliss. Producer : John O'Douglas. Screenplay : John O'Douglas, Bill Luckwell, Jack Hulbert. Photography : Kent Talbot. Production Company : Jaywell. Distributor : Adelphi. 68 minutes. Cert U.

Andrew and Kate Dax (Patrick Holt, Diana Dors) are disturbed late at night by the eccentric Miss Tulip (Cicely Courtneidge) who demands a bed, and hands over a gun and some jewellery. In the morning, she is found dead. PC Feathers (Jack Hulbert) suspects Andrew, and is about to arrest him when Miss Tulip's twin sister Angela arrives. But Andrew deduces that the newcomer is Miss Tulip who has murdered Angela for her money. Miss Tulip, now quite mad, is taken away.

Rest of Cast : A.E. Matthews. Joss Ambler. Pat Terry-Thomas. George Roderick. Brian Oulton.

A KID FOR TWO FARTHINGS (1955)

Director and Producer : Carol Reed. Screenplay : Wolf Mankowitz, from his novel. Photography : Edward Scaife. Production Company : London Films / Big Ben Films. Distributor : Independent Film Distributors / British Lion. Eastman Colour. 96 minutes. Cert U.

Publicity shot from "As Long as They're Happy"

Most of the people in London's Petticoat Lane street market have problems. – until little Joe (Jonathan Ashmore) buys a kid which, because of it's one horn, he assumes to be the unicorn of the stories told to him by tailor Kandinsky (David Kossoff). Young wrester Sam (Joe Robinson) wins a vital match and buys Sonia (Diana Dors) a ring, Kandinsky gets a new steam-press and other 'miracles' happen. The kid dies… and the boy gets a new pet.

Rest of Cast : Celia Johnson. Sidney James. Sydney Tafler. Brenda de Banzie. Primo Carnera. Vera Day. Lou Jacobi. Daphne Anderson. Harold Berens. Danny Green. Irene Handl. Rosalind Boxall. Eddie Byrne. Joseph Tomelty. Harry Purvis. Harry Baird. Lilly Kann. Arthur Lovegrove. Madge Brindley. Harold Goodwin. George Hirste. Eddie Malin. Derek Sydney. Sam Kydd. Peter Taylor. Marigold Russell. Max Denne. Norah Gordon. James Lomas. Charles Saynor. Mollie Palmer. Barbara Denney. Barbara Archer. Ann Chaplin. Anita Arley. Judith Nelmes. Arthur Skinner. Raymond Rollett. Bruce Beeby. Asher Day. Bart Allison. Norman Mitchell. Lew Mara. Frank Blake.

VALUE FOR MONEY (1955)

Director : Ken Annakin. Producer : Sergei Nolbandov. Screenplay : R.F. Delderfield, William Fairchild, from the novel by Derrick Boothroyd. Photography : Geoffrey Unsworth. Production Company : Group. Distributor : Rank. Technicolor. VistaVision. 93 minutes. Cert U.

After a spat with his girl Ethel (Susan Stephen), North Country rag millionaire Chayley (John Gregson) takes himself off to London, becoming involved with showgirl Ruthine (Diana Dors), who believes him to be poor and refuses his proposal. Discovering the truth, Ruthine rushes to accept. Chayley gets cold feet when she goes on a spending spree and although Ethel gets him back, Ruthine does get another rich Yorkshireman.

Rest of Cast : Derek Farr. Frank Pettingell. Jill Adams. Charles Victor. Donald Pleasance. Joan Hickson. Hal Osmond. Ernest Thesiger. James Gregson. Sheila Raynor. Ronald Chesney. Leslie Phillips. Paddy

Stone. Irving Davies. Sheila O'Neil. Ruth Shiel. Carol Day. Eleanor Fazan. Jane Dore. Oliver Reed. Mavis Greenaway. Julia Arnall.

AN ALLIGATOR NAMED DAISY (1955)

Director : J. Lee Thompson. Producer : Raymond Stross. Screenplay : Jack Davies, from the novel by Charles Terrot. Photography : Reginald Wyer. Production Company : Group/Raymond Stross Productions. Distributor : Rank. Technicolor. VistaVision. 88 minutes. Cert : U.

Songwriter Peter (Donald Sinden) finds himself landed with a pet alligator and Moira, an Irish girl (Jean Carson) who loves all animals. Neither of them pleases his heiress fiancée Vanessa (Diana Dors) but, after the alligator wrecks a rally designed to popularize reptiles as pets, Vanessa settles for Moira's handsome brother (Stephen Boyd) and leaves Peter, Moira and Daisy the alligator together.

Rest of Cast : James Robertson Justice. Margaret Rutherford. Stanley Holloway. Roland Culver. Avice Landone. Richard Wattis. Henry Kendall. Michael Shepley. Charles Victor. Ernest Thesiger. Wilfrid Lawson. George Moon. Jimmy Edwards. Gilbert Harding. Frankie Howerd. Martin Miller. Colin Freer. Bill Shine. Harry Green. Maurice Kaufmann. George Woodbridge. Patrick Cargill. Ronnie Stevens. Don Cameron. Arnold Bell. Charles Carson. Myrette Morven. Joan Young. John Vere.

YIELD TO THE NIGHT (1956)
(U.S.A.: Blonde Sinner)

Director : J. Lee Thompson. Producer : Kenneth Harper. Screenplay : John Cresswell, Joan Henry, from Henry's novel. Photography : Gilbert Taylor. Production Company : Associated British. Distributor : Associated British Pathe. 100 minutes. Cert : X.

Awaiting hanging for murder, Mary (Diana Dors) reflects on her past. She recalls falling in love with Jim (Michael Craig), a nightclub pianist for whom she leaves her husband. He in turn falls for another

On the set between shots for "An Alligator named Daisy" with Donald Sinden

City Suit costume design by Hardy Amies for Diana
"An Alligator Named Daisy"

woman and, when she rejects him, commits suicide. Filled with desire for revenge, Mary kills her rival. In the condemned cell, she hears that there is to be no reprieve.

Rest of Cast : Yvonne Mitchell. Geoffrey Keen. Olga Lindo. Mary Mackenzie. Joan Miller. Marie Ney. Liam Redmond. Marjorie Rhodes. Athene Seyler. Molly Urquhart. Harry Locke. Michael Ripper. Joyce Blair. Charles Clay. Peggy Livesey. Mona Washbourne. Alex Finter. Marianne Stone. Mercia Shaw. Charles Lloyd Pack. Dandy Nichols. John Charlesworth. Frank Hawkins. Shirley Ann Field.

THE UNHOLY WIFE (1957)

Director : John Farrow. Producer : John Farrow. Screenplay : Jonathan Latimer from a story by William Durkee. Photography : Lucien Ballard. Production Company :R.K.O. Radio Pictures Ltd. Distributor : R.K.O. Radio Pictures Ltd. Technicolor. 95 minutes. Cert : A.

Wealthy vintner Paul Hochen (Rod Steiger) meets blonde bombshell Phyllis (Diana Dors) in a bar... and marries her. In due course, Phyllis is bored by Paul, and finds an exciting new lover in rodeo rider San (Tom Tryon). To adjust matters, she forms a murderous scheme, which seems to be going wrong... or is it? Will irony intervene in time to thwart a seemingly perfect crime?

Rest of Cast : Beulah Bondi. Arthur Franz. Marie Windsor. Joe DeSantis. Tol Avery. Gary Hunley. James Burke. Luis Van Rooten.

THE LONG HAUL (1957)

Director : Ken Hughes. Producer : Maxwell Setton. Screenplay : Ken Hughes from the novel by Mervyn Mills. Photography : Basil Emmott. Production Company : Marksman. Distributor : Columbia. 100 minutes. Cert : A.

To please his wife (Gene Anderson) who doesn't want to go to America, ex-US army man Harry Miller (Victor Mature) becomes a truck driver. He comes up against Joe Easy (Patrick Allen), a haulage racketeer, after Joe's mistress (Diana Dors) has seduced him, and is forced to work for Joe after losing his own job. During a long haul with stolen furs, Joe is killed after a fight and Harry, shocked to find his small son dangerously ill, gives himself up.

Rest of Cast : Peter Reynolds. Liam Redmond. Meier Tzelniker. Michael Wade. Dervis Ward. Murray Kash. Jameson Clark. John Harvey. John Welsh. Roland Brand. Stanley Rose. Raymond Barry. Susan Campbell. Freddie Watts. Harcourt Curacao. Van Boolen. Norman Rossington. Martin Shaban. Madge Brindley.

I MARRIED A WOMAN (1957)

Director : Hal Kanter. Producer : William Bloom. Screenplay : Goodman Ace. Photography : Lucien Ballard. Production Company : Gomalco. Distriubtor : R.K.O. Radio Pictures Ltd. RKO-Scope Technicolor Sequence, 84 minutes. Cert : U.

Marshall Briggs (George Gobel) , of the Sutton Advertising Agency, is hard-pressed to come up with an idea to follow his successful "Miss Luxenberg" beauty contest for the Luxenberg Beer company. His original contest popularized Luxenberg Beer and led to his marriage to the winner, Janice Blake (Diana Dors). Pushed by his boss, Frederick W. Sutton (Adolph Menjou), to come up with a new idea, Marshall has neglected his wife, and his mother-in-law is suggesting to her daughter that her husband is running around on her. Meanwhile, Janice learns that she is pregnant. Marshall decides that since Janice is no longer "Miss Luxenberg" but "Mrs. Luxenberg" a great idea would be to round up all the former winners, who have married, and have a "Mrs. Luxenberg" contest.

Rest of Cast : Jessie Royce Landis. Nita Talbot. William Redfield. Stephen Dunne. John McGiver. Steve Pendleton. Stanley Adams. Suzanne Alexander. Suzanne Ames. Paul Bradley. Kay Buckley. Jeanne Carmen. Harry Cheshire. Jonathan Daly. Angie Dickinson. Joan Dixon. Bess Flowers. Paul Gary. Louise Glenn. Greg Gobel. James Gonzalez. Dick Gordon. Richard Grant. Marilyn Hanold. Marie Harmon. Sam

Harris.Don C. Harvey. Kenner G. Kemp. Sam Lee. Lou Lubin. Sidney Marion. Ann McCrea. John Wayne.

THE LOVE SPECIALIST (1958)
LA RAGAZZA DEL PALIO (Original Title)

Director : Luigi Zampa. Producer : Maleno Malenotti. Screenplay : Raffaele Gianelli. Photography : Giuseppe Rotunno. Production Company : Cite Films. Distributor : Grand National Pictures Ltd (UK). Technicolor. 84 minutes. Cert : U.

A Texan girl (Diana Dors) wins a quiz show jackpot, and uses her winnings for a trip to Italy. Her car breaks up near Siena where she meets a handsome Italian prince (Vittorio Gassman). He thinks that she must be rich, and she too believes he's loaded with cash, but they're both broke. The romance reaches its climax at the traditional Palio horse race where, after breaking up with the prince after learning that he bribed the rival jockey into throwing the race so that his horse could win, she fast-talks the rival horse's owner into letting her ride.

Rest of Cast : Franca Valeri. Bruce Cabot. Teresa Palleti. Tina Lattanzi. Enrico Viarisio. Nando Bruno. Ronaldo Bonacchi. Gianni Baghino. Nerio Bernardi. Enzo Biliotti. Giulio Cali. Frederico Collino. Cristina De Angelis.

TREAD SOFTLY STRANGER (1958)

Director : Gordon Parry. Producer : George Minter. Screenplay : George Minter, Denis O'Dell, from the play by Jack Popplewell. Photography : Douglas Slocombe. Production Company : Alderdale. Distributor : Renown. 91 minutes. Cert : A.

A Yorkshire town. Dave (Terence Morgan), who has embezzled £300 to keep his flighty girlfriend Calico (Diana Dors) in goodies, is joined by his brother Johnny (George Baker), on the run from racetrack creditors. Dave decides to solve their problems in a robbery, but he panics and kills a nightwatchman, whose son traces a missing witness, bringing a confession from Dave, who is unaware the man is blind.

Rest of Cast : Patrick Allen. Jane Griffiths. Maureen Delany. Betty Warren. Thomas Heathcote. Russell Napier. Wilfrid Lawson. Norman MacOwen. Joseph Tomelty. Chris Fay. Terry Baker. Timothy Bateson. John Salew. Michael Golden. George Merritt. Jack McNaughton. Andrew Keir. Hal Osmond. Norman Pierce. Patrick Crean. Sandra Francis.

PASSPORT TO SHAME (1958)
(USA : Room 43)

Director : Alvin Rakoff. Producer : John Clein. Screenplay : Patrick Alexander. Photography : Jack Asher. Production Company : United Co-Productions. Distributor : British Lion. 91 minutes. Cert : X.

Tricked into coming to England from France by the 'madame' (Brenda de Banzie) of a brothel and her boss, Nick (Herbert Lom), Malou (Odile Versois) believes she is being employed as a companion. Cab-driver Johnny (Eddie Constantine), with whom she has had a one-day 'marriage' to get a passport, realizes she will be coerced into prostitution, and leads London's cabbies to her rescue. Nick falls to his death from a blazing building.

Rest of Cast : Diana Dors. Robert Brown. Elwyn Brook-Jones. Cyril Shaps. Percy Cartwright. Denis Shaw. Joan Sims. James Ottaway. Lana Morris. Jackie Collins. Margaret Tyzack. Pat Pleasance. Steve Plytas. Charles Price. Robert Fabian. Michael Caine.

SCENT OF MYSTERY (1960)
(Holiday in Spain)

Director : Jack Cardiff. Producer : Mike Todd, Jr. Screenplay : Gerald Kersh. Photography : John von Kotze. Production Company : Mike Todd Company. Technicolor. 125 minutes. Cert : U.

A mystery novelist, (Denholm Elliott) discovers a plan to murder an American heiress, (Elizabeth Taylor) while on vacation in Spain.

He enlists the help of a taxi driver, (Peter Lorre), to travel across the Spanish countryside in order to thwart the crime.

Rest of Cast : Beverley Bentley. Paul Lukas. Liam Redmond. Leo Mckern. Peter Arne. Diana Dors. Mary Laura Wood. Judith Furse. Maurice Marsac. Michael Trubshawe. Juan Olaguivel. Sandra Shahan. Billie Miller.

ON THE DOUBLE (1961)

Director : Melville Shavelson. Producer : Jack Rose. Screenplay : Melville Shavelson. Jack Rose. Photography : Harry Stradling. Geoffrey Unsworth. Production Company : Dena Productions. Distributor : Paramount Film Service Ltd. Technicolor. 92 minutes. Cert : A.

Ernie Williams (Danny Kaye), a timid G. I. stationed in England shortly before the World War II Allied invasion of Normandy, is caught impersonating General Sir Lawrence Mackenzie-Smith, England's foremost battle campaigner. American and British intelligence persuade Ernie to continue the impersonation in order to confuse Nazi spies.

Rest of Cast : Dana Wynter. Wilfrid Hyde-White. Margaret Rutherford. Diana Dors. Allan Cuthbertson. Jesse White. Gregory Walcott. Terence de Marney. Rex Evans. Rudolph Anders. Edgar Barrier. Pamela Light. Ben Astar.

KING OF THE ROARING TWENTIES (1961)
(The Big Bankroll)

Director : Joseph M. Newman. Producer : Samuel Bischoff. David Diamond. Screenplay : Jo Swerling. Photography : Carl E. Guthrie. Production Company : Bischoff-Diamond Corporation. Distributor : Warner Pathe Ltd. 106 minutes. Cert : A.

Arnold Rothstein (David Janssen) gains a reputation in 1920s New York City as an expert gambler. He so impresses mob boss Big Tim

O'Brien (Jack Carson) that he is given a job in his illegal enterprises. Rothstein has a lifelong pal, Johnny Burke (Mickey Rooney), and makes a deadly enemy, Phil Butler (Dan O'Herlihy), a corrupt cop. He rises to become rich and well known in gambling circles, often using ruthless tactics, like tricking business partner Jim Kelly (Mickey Shaughnessy) into sacrificing his half of their arrangement. Although he has little time for a personal life, Rothstein impulsively marries Carolyn Green (Dianne Foster), an attractive actress. He devotes little effort to their marriage, his principal obsessions being to build a huge bankroll and to someday win a poker hand with a royal flush. As his empire grows, so does his arrogance. Rothstein eventually sells out his only friend, resulting in Burke's being gunned down by thugs. He and lawyer Tom Fowler (Keenan Wynne) conspire to make sure Butler is exposed and convicted for his criminal activities. But at the precise moment a royal flush is dealt to him, Rothstein is dealt with by Butler's associates.

Rest of Cast : Diana Dors. William Demarest. Regis Toomey. Robert Ellenstein. Tim Rooney. Murvyn Vye. Jimmy Baird. Joseph Schildkraut.

ENCONTRA A MALLORCA (1962)

Director : Jose Maria Ochoa. Production Company : Nueva Films.

No Synopsis available. The film was abandoned due to financial difficulties.

Cast : Diana Dors. Alfredo Kraus. George Rigaud.

MRS GIBBONS' BOYS (1962)

Director : Max Varnel. Producer : Henry Halstead. Screenplay : Peter Blackmore. Max Varnel. Photography : Stanley Pavey (as Stan Pavey). Production Company : Henry Halstead Productions. Distributor : Byron Films Ltd. 82 minutes. Cert : A.

An ageing widow (Kathleen Harrison) finally finds new love and

King of the Roaring Twenties
Dianne Foster as Carolyn with Diana as Madge

happiness; but matters are complicated when her two convict sons escape from prison and beg her to hide them.

Rest of Cast : Lionel Jeffries. Diana Dors. John Le Mesurier. Frederick Bartman. David Lodge. Dick Emery. Eric Pohlmann. William Kerwin. Milo O'Shea. Peter Hempson. Penny Morrell. Nancy Nevinson. Mark Singleton. Tony Hilton.

WEST 11 (1963)

Director : Michael Winner. Producer : Daniel M. Angel. Screenplay : Willis Hall, Keith Waterhouse from a play by Laura del Rivo. Photography : Otto Heller. Production Company : Angel Productions (Dial Films Ltd). Distributor : Dial Films Ltd. 93 minutes. Cert : X.

In Notting Hill's jazz club, coffee bar and bedsit land of the early 1960s, Joe Beckett (Alfred Lynch) is a young unemployed misfit and drifter whose life takes a turn for the worse when he encounters Richard Dyce (Eric Portman), an ex-army veteran. Dyce persuades Beckett it will be in his interests to bump off Dyce's wealthy aunt (Marie Ney) for her money. Beckett travels to the old lady's house on the South coast, and prepares to murder her, but loses his nerve and in a struggle, accidentally pushes her down a flight of stairs, killing her anyway. After a witness (Harold Lang) reports him, Beckett returns to his digs and finds the police waiting for him. Dyce denies all involvement and Beckett panics and turns himself in.

Rest of Cast : Kathleen Breck. Diana Dors. Kathleen Harrison. Finlay Currie. Freda Jackson. Peter Reynolds. Allan McClelland. Francesca Annis. Gerry Duggan. Sean Kelly. Patrick Wymark.

THE COUNTERFEIT CONSTABLE (1964)
Allez France! (Original Title)

Director : Robert Dhéry. Pierre Tchernia. Producer : Henri Diamant-Berger. Screenplay : Colette Brosset. Robert Dhéry. Jean Lhote.

Pierre Tcherina. Photography : Jean Tournier. Production Company : Compagnie Industrielle et Commerciale Cinématographique (CICC) Distributor : Gala Film Distributors Ltd. Eastmancolor 90 minutes. Cert : U.

On the eve of his wedding and unbeknownst to his fiancée (Catherine Sola), Henri (Robert Dhery) attended the England-France rugby match at Twickenham . An English supporter breaks two of his teeth during the meeting, and Henri is treated by a dentist of London (Colin Gordon) who asks him to stay two hours without opening his mouth. Meanwhile, the dentist has to take care of a policeman (Bernard Cribbins) who left in the locker room, helmet and uniform. To pass the time, Henri takes the uniform and leaves, rescuing a glamorous film star (Diana Dors) from the grip of a maniac who is about to shoot her. Then begins the burlesque adventures of Henri, an alleged but silent policeman in the English capital. Wanted by an ever-increasing number of people, he tries to solve his problem with difficulty and find his way back to the dentist.

Rest of Cast : Pierre Tornade. Pierre Doris. Raymond Bussiéres. Jean Richard. Mark Lester. Ronald Fraser. Colette Brosset. Arthur Mullard. Percy Herbert. Amy Dalby. Robert Burnier. Richard Vernon. Colin Blakely.

THE SANDWICH MAN (1966)

Director : Robert Hartford-Davis. Producer : Peter Newbrook. Screenplay : Michael Bentine. Robert Hartford-Davis. Photography : Peter Newbrook. Production Company : Titan International Pictures. Distributor : Rank Film Distributors Lrd. Eastmancolor. 95 minutes. Cert : U

Horace Quilby (Michael Bentine), is a mild-mannered widower living in the London Docklands. His job as a sandwich-board man requires him to wander around London wearing morning dress and carrying advertisements. He is also secretary of the Sandwichmen's Brotherhood. But his real interest in life is pigeon racing, especially 'Esmerelda', who is racing from Bordeaux to London. During the

"The Conterfeit Constable" with Robert Dhéry

course of one day, Quilby encounters a host of eccentric characters, who are played by some of Britain's best known comedy and character actors, and becomes involved in a series of capers. The main story thread sees Quilby reunite Sue (Suzy Kendall), a young model with Steven (David Buck), her errant boyfriend. Esmerelda wins her race, and the whole of Quilby's neighbourhood join in the celebrations.

Rest of Cast : Dora Bryan. Harry H. Corbett. Bernard Cribbins. Diana Dors. Ian Hendry. Stanley Holloway. Wilfrid Hyde-White. Michael Medwin. Ron Moody. Anna Quayle. Terry -Thomas. Norman Wisdom. Donald Wolfit..

BERSERK! (1967)

Director : Jim O'Connolly. Producer : Herman Cohen. Screenplay : Aben Kandel. Herman Cohen. Photography : Desmond Dickinson. Production Company : Herman Cohen Productions. Distributor : Columbia Picture Corporation Lrd. Technicolor. 96 minutes. Cert : X.

As the co-owner and ringmaster of a travelling circus, Monica Rivers (Joan Crawford) is always preoccupied with filling seats. Following the accidental death of a tightrope walker, Rivers is pleased to see her profits increase and callously unconcerned with the demise of her employee, and soon hires handsome Frank Hawkins (Ty Hardin) to replace him. But when several more performers meet gruesome deaths, it becomes apparent they are no accidents, and there's a killer on the loose.

Rest of Cast : Diana Dors. Michael Gough. Judy Geeson. Robert Hardy. Geoffrey Keen. Sydney Tafler. George Claydon. Philip Madoc. Ambosine Phillpotts. Thomas Cimarro. Peter Burton. Golda Casimir. Ted Lune.

DANGER ROUTE (1967)

Director : Seth Holt. Producer : Milton Subotsky. Max Rosenberg. Screenplay : Meade Roberts. Robert Banks Stewart. From a novel by Andrew York. Photography : Harry Waxman. Production Company :

Amicus. Distributor : United Artists Corporation Lrd. DeLuxe Color. 92 minutes. Cert :A.

Returning from a mission in the Caribbean, Jonas Wilde (Richard Johnson) is determined it will be his last. Coaxed by his superiors into one more dirty assassination job, mid-way through this mission Wilde discovers a plot to kill agents emanating from within British Security Service itself.

Rest of Cast : Carol Lynley. Barbara Bouchet. Sylvia Syms. Gordon Jackson. Diana Dors. Maurice Denham. Sam Wanamaker. David Bauer. Robin Bailey. Harry Andrews. Julian Chagrin. Reg Lye. Leslie Sands. Timothy Bateson.

HAMMERHEAD (1968)

Director : David Miller. Producer : Irving Allen. Screenplay : William Bast. Herbert Baker. From a novel by James Mayo. John Briley (Adaptation). Photography :Wilkie Cooper. Kenneth Talbot. Production Company : Irving Allen Productions. Distributor : Irving Allen Ltd. Technicolor. 100 minutes. Cert : A.

American secret agent Charles Hood (Vince Edwards) is instructed by Colonel Condor (Patrick Cargill) of British Security to trap Hammerhead (Peter Vaughan), an international criminal and collector of erotic art who is suspected of wanting to steal a secret report on a nuclear defense system presented at a NATO conference in Lisbon. By offering to sell a priceless collection of pornography, Hood gets himself invited aboard Hammerhead's yacht, but his sleuthing is hampered by the attentiveness of Sue Trenton (Judy Geeson), a model and nightclub entertainer, and the seductive advances of Hammerhead's mistress, Ivory (Beverly Adams). Hood finally uncovers Hammerhead's scheme to kidnap Sir Richard Calvert, Britain's NATO delegate, and replace him at the conference with Andreas (Michael Bates), a professional impersonator formerly employed at a nightclub owned by Kit (Diana Dors), another of Hammerhead's mistresses.

Rest of Cast : Patrick Holt. William Mervyn. Douglas Wilmer. Tracy

Richard Johnson as Jonas Wilde and Diana as Rhoda Gooderich

"Hammerhead" as Kit

Reed. Kenneth Cope. Kathleen Byron. Jack Woolgar. Joseph Furst. Andreas Malandrinos. David Prowse. Earl Younger. Romo Gorrara. Maggie Wright. Veronica Carlson. Penny Brahms. Sarah Hardenberg. Otto Diamant. Windsor Davies. Arthur Gomez.

BABY LOVE (1968)

Director : Alastair Reid. Producer : Guido Coen. Screenplay : Alastair Reid. Guido Coen. Michael Klinger from a novel by Tina Chad Christian. Photography : Desmond Dickinson. Production Company : Avton Films. Distributor : Avton Films. Eastmancolor. 93 minutes. Cert : X

After her impoverished, cancer-ridden mother (Diana Dors) commits suicide, schoolgirl Luci (Linda Hayden) is adopted by her mother's ex-lover Robert (Keith Barron), now a wealthy, married doctor living the high-life in London. Once in her new home, the deeply-disturbed girl gradually spirals out of control.

Rest of Cast : Ann Lynn. Sheila Steafel. Dick Emery. Lewis Wilson. Derek Lamden. Patience Collier. Terence Brady. Marianne Stone. Christine Pryor. Yvonne Horner. Vernon Dobtcheff. Troy Dante.

THERE'S A GIRL IN MY SOUP (1970)

Director : Roy Boulting. Producer : John Boulting. Screenplay : Terence Frisby from his stage play. Peter Kortner (additional dialogue). Photography : Harry Waxman. Production Company : Charter Film Productions. Distributor : Columbia Pictures Corporation Ltd. Eastmancolor. 96 minutes. Cert : X.

Robert Danvers (Peter Sellers), is a vain, womanizing and wealthy host of a high-profile cooking show. He meets Marion (Goldie Hawn), a no-nonsense American hippie living with an English rock musician in London, and, to everyone's surprise, falls for her She moves in with him, and accompanies him on a trip to a wine festival in France.

Meanwhile, her rock musician boyfriend Jimmy (Nicky Henson) decides he wants her back.

Rest of Cast : Tony Britton. Ruth Trouncer. Francoise Pascal. Geraldine Sherman. Tom Marshall. John Comer. Diana Dors. Nicola Pagett. Judy Campbell. Gabrielle Drake. Raf De Le Torre. Constantine Gregory.

DEEP END (1970)

Director : Jerzy Skolimowski. Producer : Helmut Jedele. Screenplay : Jerzy Skolimowski. Jerzy Gruza. Boleslaw Sulik. Photography : Charly Steinberger. Production Company : Maran Film. Kettledrum Productions. Distributor : Kettledrum Films. Eastmancolor. 91 minutes. Cert : X.

Mike (John Moulder-Brown), a 15-year-old public baths attendant, develops a crush on his older, attractive co-worker, Susan (Jane Asher). At first they help each other secure bigger tips by swapping their respective male and female clients. But their tidy business arrangement is severed when Mike discovers that Susan has not only shunned him, but is cheating on her fiancé (Christopher Sandford) with an older man (Karl Michael Vogler). As Mike begins stalking Susan in an effort to break them up, his innocent crush spirals into obsession.

Rest of Cast : Diana Dors. Louise Martini. Erica Beer. Anita Lochner. Anne-Marie Kuster. Cheryl Hall. Christine Paul-Podlasky. Dieter Eppler. Karl Ludwig Lindt. Eduard Linkers. Will Danin. Gerald Rowland. Berk Kwouk.

HANNIE CAULDER (1971)

Director : Burt Kennedy. Producer : Patrick Curtis. Screenplay : Burt Kennedy. David Haft. Photography : Edward Scaife. Production Company : Curtwell Productions. Paramount Pictures. Tigon British Film Productions. Distributor : Continental Films. Cert : AA.

In the Wild West, vicious but bumbling bandit brothers Emmett (Ernest Borgnine), Frank (Jack Elam) and Rufus Clemens (Strother Martin) botch a heist, and in anger they rape local woman Hannie Caulder (Raquel Welch), murder her spouse and destroy her home. Set on retribution, Hannie seeks out bounty hunter Thomas Luther Price (Robert Culp), who helps her learn to shoot – a skill that she'll need as she attempts to track down and take out the merciless Clemens brothers.

Rest of Cast : Christopher Lee. Diana Dors. Florencia Amanilla. Luis Barboo. Stephen Boyd. Paco de Lucia. Brian Lightburn. Aldo Sambrell.

THE PIED PIPER (1972)

Director : Jacques Demy. Producer : Sanford Lieberson. David Puttnam. Screenplay : Mark Peplow. Andrew Birkin. Jacques Demy. Photography : Peter Suschitzky.. Production Company : Sagittarious Productions Inc. Goodtimes Enterprises. Distributor : Scotia Barber. Eastmancolor. 86 minutes. Cert : A.

A caravan of performers travels to Hamelin, Germany, to celebrate the marriage of Franz (John Hurt) to the burgomaster's ailing daughter, Lisa (Cathryn Harrison). Fearing that they carry the plague, however, the townsfolk will not let them in until it is discovered that the music played by the group's piper (Donovan) has cured Lisa. Once inside, the piper strikes a deal with the burgomaster (Roy Kinnear) to also rid the town of rats. But when the piper doesn't receive his due, he exacts a terrible revenge.

Rest of Cast : Keith Buckley. Patsy Puttnam. Arthur Hewlett. Paul Hennen. Peter Eyre. David Leland. Michael Hordern. Jack Wild. Michael Goldie. Diana Dors. Cathryn Harrison. Peter Vaughan. Andre Van Gysegham.

SWEDISH WILDCATS (1972)
Every Afternoon (Original Title)

Director : Joseph W. Sarno. Producer : Vernon P. Becker. Screenplay

: Vernon P. Becker. Joseph W. Sarno. Photography : Lasse Bjorne. Production Company : Unicorn Enterprises. Distributor : Atlantic Film Distributors Ltd. Colour. 85 minutes. Cert : X.

The sadistic Madam Margareta (Diana Dors) is the hostess and ring leader for a live sex tease show and whorehouse. Madam's shows always feature her bodacious nieces Susanna (Cia Löwgren) and Karen (Solveig Andersson), who perform in everything from striptease to S&M acts. Karen meets and eventually runs away with a rich guy. Susanna falls in love with a deceptive airport cargo handler (Peder Kinberg). After several more kinky shows and various soft core sex scenes, Karen is gone and Susanna and her man find out the truth behind each others lies.

Rest of Cast : Ib Mossin. John Harryson. Christina Lindberg. Urban Standar. Egil Holmsen. Claes Thelander. Alan Lake. Sven-Olaf Eriksson. Jan Rohde. Poul Glargaard. Marie-Louise Fors.

THE AMAZING MR. BLUNDEN (1972)

Director : Lionel Jeffries. Producer : Barry Levinson. Screenplay :Lionel Jeffries. Antonia Barber (Novel). Photography :Gerry Fisher. Production Company : Hemdale. Distributor : Hemisphere Productions. Eastmancolor. 99 minutes. Cert : U.

A widow (Dorothy Alison) and her two children (Lynne Frederick & Garry Miller) are visited by a mysterious solicitor (Laurence Naismith), who offers her a job as caretaker of a derelict mansion. The youngsters discover the house is haunted by two children (Rosalyn Landor & Marc Granger) and try to lay the ghosts to rest, ultimately using magic to travel back to when they died.

Rest of Cast : Graham Crowden. Benamin Smith. Stuart Lock. Deddie Davies. David Lodge. Madeline Smith. James Villiers. Diana Dors. Erik Chitty.

STEPTOE AND SON RIDE AGAIN (1973)

Director : Peter Sykes. Producer : Aida Young. Screenplay : Ray Galton.

Alan Simpson. Photography : Ernest Steward. Production Company : Associated London Films. Distributor : Hammer Film Distributors Ltd. Technicolor. 99 minutes. Cert: A.

Albert Steptoe (Wilfrid Brambell) and his son Harold (Harry H. Corbett) are junk dealers, complete with horse and cart to tour the neighbourhood. They also live together at the junk yard. Always on the lookout for ways to improve his lot, Harold invests his father's life savings in a greyhound who is almost blind and can't see the hare. When the dog loses a race and Harold has to pay off the debt, he comes up with another bright idea. Collect his father's life insurance. To do this his father must pretend to be dead.

Rest of Cast : Diana Dors. Milo O'Shea. Neil McCarthy. Bill Maynard. George Tovey. Sam Kydd. Yootha Joyce. Olga Lowe. Joyce Hemson. Henry Woolf. Geoffrey Bayldon. Frank Thornton. Richard Davies.

THEATRE OF BLOOD (1973)
USA : Theater of Blood

Director : Douglas Hickox. Producer : John Kohn. Stanley Mann. Screenplay : Anthony Greville-Bell. Photography : Wolfgang Suschitzky. Production Company: Harbour Productions Limited. Cineman Productions. Distributor : Cineman Films Ltd. Colour. 104 minutes. Cert : X

After being humiliated at an awards ceremony, Shakespearean actor Edward Lionheart (Vincent Price) commits suicide by diving into the Thames. Unbeknownst to the public, he survives and is rescued by a group of vagrants. Two years later, on March 15th, Lionheart sets out to exact vengeance against the critics who failed to salute his genius.

Rest of Cast : Diana Rigg. Ian Hendry. Harry Andrews. Coral Browne. Robert Coote. Jack Hawkins. Michael Hordern. Arthur Lowe. Robert Morley. Dennis Price. Milo O'Shea. Eric Sykes. Madeline Smith. Diana Dors.

Harry H Corbett as Harold Steptoe with Diana in
"Steptoe and Son Ride Again"

NOTHING BUT THE NIGHT (1973)

Director : Peter Sasdy. Producer : Anthony Nelson Keys. Screenplay : Brian Hayes from a novel by John Blackburn. Photography : Kenneth Talbot. Production Company : Charlemagne Productions. Distributor: Rank Film Distributors Ltd. Eastmancolor. 90 minutes. Cert : AA.

When various trustees of the Van Traylen Orphanage begin dying in close order, it's at first written off as a coincidence. But, when a school bus accident very nearly takes out three more of them along with a group of orphans, Col. Bingham (Christopher Lee) and his pathologist friend, Mark (Peter Cushing), begin looking into the deaths. They come to think the answer lies with one of the girls on the bus, who has vivid memories of things she could not possibly have seen.

Rest of Cast : Diana Dors. Georgia Brown. Keith Barron. Gwyneth Strong. Fulton Mackay. John Robinson. Morris Perry. Michael Gambon. Shelagh Fraser. Duncan Lamont. Kathleen Byron. Geoffrey Frederick. Louise Nelson.

FROM BEYOND THE GRAVE (1974)

Director : Kevin Connor. Producer : Max Rosenberg. Milton Subotsky. Screenplay : Robin Clarke. Raymond Christodoulou. Photography : Alan Hume. Production Company : Amicus Productions. Distributor : Columbia-Warner Distribtuors. Technicolor. 97 minutes. Cert : X.

If anyone cheats the shop's proprieter (Peter Cushing) at Temptations Ltd, a nasty fate awaits them. Four customers purchase items:- (1.) The Gatecrasher: Edward Charlton (David Warner) tricks the proprieter into believing an antique mirror is a reproduction in order to get a lower price. After Edward holds a seance, a mysterious figure appears in the mirror. (2.) An Act of Kindness: Christopher Lowe (Ian Bannen), a bored office worker and henpecked husband, befriends a match and shoelace seller, Jim Underwood (Donald Pleasence). Christopher finds that Jim is a decorated soldier, and in an attempt to impress him tries to buy a war medal from the antique shop proprieter. Not having the required paperwork to purchase the medal, he instead steals it. After ingratiating himself with Lowe, he finds that the old soldier is less innocent than he at first thought. (3.) The Elemental: After tricking the proprieter into buying a cheap snuff box, Reggie Warren (Ian Carmichael), a pompous businessman, boards a train. On the train a woman known as Madame Orloff (Margaret Leighton) informs him that he has an Elemental on his shoulder. When he gets back to his house, he discovers that the Elemental has followed him there. (4.) The Door: William Seaton (Ian Ogilvy), a writer, buys an antique door from the proprieter. When he takes it back home, he finds that a mysterious blue room lies behind the door. It begins to exert such a strong influence over him that it threatens his very soul.

Rest of Cast: Diana Dors. Nyree Dawn Porter. Angela Pleasence. Lesley-Anne Down. Jack Watson. Wendy Allnutt. Rosalind Ayres. Tommy Godfrey.

CRAZE (1974)
The Infernal Idol

Director : Freddie Francis. Producer : Herman Cohen. Screenplay : Aben Kandel. Herman Cohen. Photography : John Wilcox. Production Company : Harbour Productions Limited. Distributor : EMI Distributors. Technicolor 96 minutes. Cert : X

The story follows the murderous activities of antique shop owner Neal Mottram (Jack Palance) as he carries out human sacrifices in the name of the African God Chuku who he believes will reward him with great wealth in return for his services. As he adopts increasingly creative methods against his female victims, will anyone be able to put a stop to his mad rituals?

Rest of Cast : Diana Dors. Julie Ege. Edith Evans. Hugh Griffith. Trevor Howard. Michael Jayston. Suzy Kendall. Martin Potter. Percy Herbert. David Warbeck. Kathleen Byron. Marianne Stone. Dean Harris.

THE AMOROUS MILKMAN (1975)

Director : Derren Nesbitt. Producer : Derren Nesbitt. Screenplay :

Derren Nesbitt. Photography: James Allen. Production Company : Lactifer Films. Distributor : Lanka Films. Colour 86 minutes. Cert : X

Milkman Davey (Brendan Price) bites off more than he can chew when he starts to deliver more than pints of milk to some of the bored housewives on his round.

Rest of Cast : Julie Ege. Diana Dors. Donna Reading. Nancie Wait. Alan Lake. Bill Fraser. Fred Emney. Patrick Holt. Roy Kinnear. Ray Barrett. Anthony Sharp. Megs Jenkins. Arnold Ridley. Sam Kydd.

WHAT THE SWEDISH BUTLER SAW (1975)
A Man with a Maid

Director : Vernon P. Becker. Producer : Inge Ivarson. Screenplay : Vernon P. Becker. Barry E. Downes. Photography : Tony Forsberg. Production Company : Film AB Robur. Unicorn Enterprises. Distributor :Entertainment Film Distributors Ltd Eastmancolor 83 minutes. Cert : X

A Victorian aristocrat Jack Armstrong (Ollie Soltoft) buys a former madhouse and converts it into a love nest. He intends to seduce Alice, the object of his desire, but is unaware that Jack the Ripper (Martin Young) lives in the secret passages lining the building. After receiving the help of a brothel madame (Diana Dors) he tries to seduce Alice (Sue Longhurst) with hypnotism, aphrodisiacs and various seduction devices. All his efforts though end in hilarious disaster as this saucy 1970's romp unfolds. Eventually Jack gets more than he bargained for as Alice turns the tables on him and reveals the true hot blooded woman under her prim exterior.

Rest of Cast : Charlie Elvegård. Malou Cartwright. Göthe Grefbo. Steven Lund. Larry Leonard. Par-Axel Arosenius. Julie Bernby. Borje Mellvig. Nils Eklund. Barbro Hiort af Ornäs. Egil Holmsen.

BEDTIME WITH ROSIE (1975)

Director : Wolf Rilla. Producer : Michael Fenton. Wolf Rilla. Screenplay : Ivor Burgoyne. Photography : Mark McDonald. Production Company

Brendan Price as Davey with Diana as Rita

:London International Films. Distributor : London International Film Distributors. Colour 80 minutes. Cert : AA.

Rosie (Una Stubbs) is a pretty, confused and pregnant young woman. She is planning a new life for herself in Holland. En route from Liverpool she presents herself unannounced on the doorstep of her Aunt's London home in search of a bed for the night. The buxom Aunt (Diana Dors) is delighted to see her but is dubious about the reaction to Rosie's overnight stay from the lodger Harry (Ivor Burgoyne), a forty year old bachelor of high moral principles. As expected Harry is hostile to the idea of sharing his room with Rosie but during the course of their bedtime chatting a relationship begins to develop.

Rest of Cast : Johnny Briggs. Margaret Lewis. Ned Lynch. Tony Doonan. Nicky Henson.

THREE FOR ALL (1975)

Director : Martin Campbell. Producer : Tudor Gates. Harold Shampan. Screenplay : Tudor Gates. Harold Shampan (screen story). Photography : Ian Wilson. Production Company : Dejamus. Distributor : Fox-Rank. Eastmancolor 89 minutes. Cert : U.

Three girls (Adrienne Posta, Cheryl Hall, Lesley North) follow their pop singer boyfriends on a tour of Spain desperately trying to catch up with them whilst getting involved in all sorts of trouble along the way.

Rest of Cast : Graham Bonnet. Robert Lindsay. Paul Nicholas. Christopher Neil. Richard Beckinsale. George Baker. Simon Williams. Cathy Collins. Diana Dors. Jonathan Adams. Arthur Mullard. Sheila Bernette.

ADVENTURES OF A TAXI DRIVER (1976)

Director : Stanley Long. Producer : Peter Long. Stanley Long. Screenplay : Suzanne Mercer. Photography : Peter Sinclair. Production Company : Salon Productions. Distributor : Icon Film Distribution. Colour 89 minutes. Cert: X

Ivor Burgoyne as Harry, Diana as Aunt Annie, and Una Stubbs
as Rosie in "Bedtime with Rosie"

Young cabbie Joe (Barry Evans) walks out on his mother (Diana Dors) and fiancé (Adrienne Posta) and has no trouble picking up young girls, working as a randy London cabbie. He also sets his sights on his best mate's bird (Judy Geeson). Joe is after anything in a skirt using his charm and cockiness to get the girls into his bed and subsequently ending up on top. Unfortunately for him he picks up a transvestite client (Stephen Riddle) and gets more than he bargained for. He then gets into a whole lot of trouble when his fare turns out to be a gang of jewel thieves needing a getaway driver.

Rest of Cast : Liz Fraser. Jane Hayden. Ian Lavender. Stephen Lewis. Robert Lindsay. Henry McGee. Angela Scoular. Brian Wilde. Marc Harrison. Graham Ashley. Dave Carter.

KEEP IT UP DOWNSTAIRS (1976)

Director : Robert Young. Producer : Hazel Adair. Screenplay : Hazel Adair. Photography : Alan Pudney. Production Company : Pyramid. Distributor : Thorn EMI. Technicolor 94 minutes. Cert : X.

The year is 1904, and the setting is Cockshute Towers, one of England's Stateliest Homes. Earl Cockshute (Mark Singleton) is faced with a grave dilemma: the debts of the once-great family have been bought by Snotty Shuttleworth (William Rushton), a local villager who ventured to Australia and made his fortune in trade. Now he is back in England, and fancies himself as Lord if they cannot pay what they owe within a month.

Rest of Cast : Jack Wild. Sue Longhurst. Olivia Munday. Diana Dors. John Blythe. Seretta Wilson. Peter Halliday. Craig Marriott. Julian Orchard. Aimi MacDonald. Carmen Silvera. Nigel Pegram. April Olrich. Mary Millington.

ADVENTURES OF A PRIVATE EYE (1977)

Director : Stanley Long. Producer : Peter Long. Stanley Long. Screenplay : Michael Armstrong. Photography: Peter Sinclair. Production

Barry Evans as Joe with Diana as Mrs North

Company : Salon Productions. Distributor : Icon Film Distribution. Gevacolor 96 minutes. Cert : X

Bob West (Christopher Neil) is the young assistant to top private detective Judd Blake (Jon Pertwee). While his boss is away carrying out some very 'private' investigations, Bob gets his first case. A beautiful model Laura Sutton (Suzy Kendall), is being blackmailed for £50,000. She must get back some compromising nude photographs or forfeit her huge inheritance.

Rest of Cast : Harry H. Corbett. Diana Dors. Fred Emney. Liz Fraser. Irene Handl. Ian Lavender. Julian Orchard. Adrienne Posta. Anna Quayle. William Rushton. Robin Stewart. Veronica Doran.

CONFESSIONS FROM THE DAVID GALAXY AFFAIR (1979)

Director : Willy Roe. Producer : Willy Roe. Screenplay : George Evans. Photography : Douglas Hill. Production Company : Roldvale Distributor : Tigon Film Distributors. Colour 97 minutes. Cert : X.

Professional astrologer and lothario David Galaxy (Alan Lake), finds himself entangled with the Law and must be able to provide an alibi to clear himself from an incident that involved robbery and murder five years previously.

Rest of Cast : Glynn Edwards. Anthony Booth. Diana Dors. John Moulder-Brown. Milton Reid. Bernie Winters. Kenny Lynch. Mary Millington. Sally Faulkner. Rosemary England. Queenie Watts. Cindy Truman. Vicki Scott. Alec Mango.

STEAMING (1985)

Director : Joseph Losey. Producer : Paul Mills. Screenplay : Nell Dunn (from her stage play). Robin Bextor (additional narrative). Patricia Losey. Photography : Christopher Challis. Production Company : World Film Services. Distributor : Columbia-EMI-Warner. Colour 95 minutes. Cert : 18.

This is a story of a group of women overcoming several obstacles by helping each other out, even if that means just listening. Seven different women whose backgrounds are filled in by flashbacks and narration are together at a women-only steam baths. Violet (Diana Dors) is the maternal manager of the establishment, and one of the issues to be resolved is how to save the baths from being shut down by the authorities.

Rest of Cast : Vanessa Redgrave. Sarah Miles. Patti Love. Brenda Bruce. Felicity Dean. Sally Sagoe. Anna Tzelniker.

Discography

DIANA DORS TF 506

So Little Time

Side One: **SO LITTLE TIME**
    (L.Reed/B.Mason)

Side Two: **IT'S TOO LATE**
    (L.Reed/B.Mason)

With arrangement directed by: **Les Reed**

Recording first published 1964

This high fidelity FONTANA record should be played at 45 r.p.m. Handle with care. Prevent damage by ensuring that you use the correct stylus, that the stylus is not worn, and that the surface of the disc is regularly cleaned. Do not touch the grooves with the finger and avoid exposure to heat and dust.

WARNING—Copyright subsists in all Fontana recordings. Any unauthorised broadcasting, public performance, copying or re-recording of Fontana records in any manner whatsoever will constitute an infringement of such copyright. Licences for the use of records for public performances may be obtained from Phonographic Performance Limited, 356-366 Oxford Street, London, W.1.

A PRODUCT OF PHILIPS   Printed and made in Great Britain

SINGLES

I Feel So Mmm…/A Kiss and a Cuddle
    Recorded in London, November 10 1953
    His Master's Voice, 1954 10613
April Heart / Point of No Return
    Pye Records, January 1960 7N.15242
So Little Time / It's Too Late
    Fontana, 1964 TF 506 267390 TF
    Fontana, 19 April 2014 (Record Store Day) 377 599-9
Security / Gary
    Polydor Records, 23 September 1966 56111
Passing By / It's A Small World
    EMI 14 October 1977 EMI 2705
Where Did They Go? / It's You Again (with son Gary)
    Nomis Records, 5 December 1981. NOM 1

ALBUMS

As Long As They're Happy – Film Soundtrack
    HMV 1954 DLPC1 (Vinyl)
    Sepia 21 May 2007 5055122110927 (CD)
Swingin' Dors
    Pye Records 1960 NPL18044 (Red Vinyl)
    Columbia 1960 CL1436 (Black Vinyl)
    Conifer 1986 CFRC501 (Vinyl)
    Conifer 1986 CFRP 501 (Picture Disc)
    Conifer 1986 MCFRC501 (Cassette)
    Sanctuary Records 2007 CMFCD1554 (CD)
    Castle Music 2007 NPL18044 Limited Edition Red Vinyl, (Numbered)
    Hallmark Music & Entertainment 2012 712432 (CD)
    Poppydisc 19 April 2014 (Record Store Day) POPPYLP023 (Red Vinyl)

Thoroughly Modern Millie
    World Record Club 1968 T849 (Vinyl)
Doctor Dolittle
    World Record Club 1968 ST851 T850(Stereo) (Vinyl)
Va-Va-Voom!
Screen Sirens Sing!
    Rhino Records 1985 RNTA 1999
Music For A Bachelor's Den Volume 7
Sex Kittens in Hi – Fi – The Blondes
    DCC Compact Classics 1996 DZS-097
Under the Influence – Morrisey
    Disco Mix Club 2003 UTILP 001 (Vinyl)
    Disco Mix Club 2003 UTICD 001 (CD)
The Girls Are At It Again : UK Beat Girls 1964-1969
    Universal Music August 2009 0-06024-9841094-3 (CD)
Bombshells : Singing Sirens of the Silver Screen
    Fantastic Voyage 2011 FVDD122 (CD)
It's a Scandal! Songs for Soho Blondes
    Fantastic Voyage November 18 2013 FVCD180 (CD)
Sixties Girls
    Not Now Music 2014 NOT3CD 160 (CD)
Bombshells & Pin Ups : Silver Screen Sirens
    Union Square Music 2015 METRTN083 (CD)

Photographic Acknowledgements

The author and publishers would like to express their appreciation of all the photographers who worked with Diana Dors over the years. All illustrations reproduced here are in the spirit of publicity, and whilst every effort has been made to trace the copyright owners, the author and publishers apologise for any omissions, and will undertake to make any appropriate changes in future editions of the book, if necessary.

Unless otherwise stated ★ all pictures are from the author's personal collection.

Paul Sullivan. (Diana Dors Personal Collection) ★   page 41

Paul Sullivan (Diana Dors Personal Collection) ★   page 42

London Film Productions   page 44

Hammer Films. Lippert Films   page 48

Mirrorpic   page 50

John Hardman. Film Studios Manchester   page 57

Ralph Conway   page 60

Associated British Pathe Limited   page 65

Associated British Pathe Limited   page 66

Jaywell. Adelphi Films Limited   page 68

Jaywell. Adelphi Films Limited   page 69

London Films   page 71

Norman Gryspeerdt. Group Film Productions Limited   page 74

Norman Gryspeerdt. Group Film Productions Limited   page 75

George Higgins. Kenwood Productions   page 81

George Higgins. Kenwood Productions   page 85

Gomalco Productions   page 92

Gomalco Productions   page 94

Treasure Productions   page 99

Treasure Productions   page 103

Paul Popper Limited   page 104

Marksman Productions Ltd. Warwick Film Productions   page 108

Edward Quinn   page 112

Cite Films. G.E.S.I. Cinematografica. Olimpo   page 116

George Minter Prodcutions. (Alderdale)   page 119

George Minter Productions (Alderdale)   page 120

United Co-Productions   page 122

Television Products Ltd   page 129

George Higgins. Angel Productions (Dial)   page 134

George Higgins. Angel Productions (Dial)   page 135

ABC Television   page 137

Herman Cohen Productions   page 142

Avton Films   page 144

Gilloon Agency   page 148

Yorkshire Television   page 155

Hemdale. Hemisphere Productions Ltd   page 160

Index